Tourist Dollars Fueling Growth in Local Economies

Tourist Dollars Fueling Growth in Local Economies

RAFEAL MECHLORE

WSM Publisher

CONTENTS

INDEX   1

INTRODUCTION   3

1 | Chapter 1   18

2 | Chapter 2   43

3 | Chapter 3   68

4 | Chapter 4   92

5 | Chapter 5   114

6 | Chapter 6   137

7 | Chapter 7   160

8 | Chapter 8   180

9 | Chapter 9   204

10 | Chapter 10   227

INDEX

Introduction

1. The Importance of Tourism
1. Defining Tourism
2. Tourism's Global Impact

B. Purpose and Scope of the Book
C. Overview of Chapters

Chapter 1: Understanding the Tourist Economy
1.1 The Tourist Economy Defined
1.2 Key Components of the Tourist Economy
1.3 Benefits of Tourism
1.4 Challenges of Tourism
1.5 Economic Models in Tourism

Chapter 2: The Local Economic Impact
2.1 Local Economies and Tourism
2.2 Measuring Economic Impact
2.3 Job Creation and Local Development
2.4 Infrastructure Development

Chapter 3: Tourism and Small Businesses
3.1 Role of Small Businesses in Tourism
3.2 Support Systems for Small Businesses
3.3 Success Stories of Small Businesses in Tourist Areas
3.4 Challenges Small Businesses Face

Chapter 4: Sustainable Tourism

4.1 Principles of Sustainable Tourism
4.2 Balancing Economic Growth with Environmental Conservation
4.3 Community Engagement in Sustainable Tourism

Chapter 5: Tourism and Cultural Preservation
5.1 The Intersection of Tourism and Culture
5.2 Cultural Attractions and Tourism
5.3 Protecting and Promoting Local Cultures
5.4 The Impact of Cultural Tourism on Local Economies

Chapter 6: Infrastructure Development and Tourism
6.1 Transportation and Accessibility
6.2 Accommodations and Tourism
6.3 Public Services and Tourism
6.4 Infrastructure Investments and Returns

Chapter 7: Marketing and Promotion
7.1 The Role of Marketing in Attracting Tourists
7.2 Online and Offline Marketing Strategies
7.3 Public-Private Partnerships in Tourism Promotion

Chapter 8: The Role of Government
8.1 Government Policies and Tourism
8.2 Regulation and Oversight
8.3 Tourism Promotion Agencies
8.4 Taxation and Tourism

Chapter 9: Challenges and Controversies
9.1 Over tourism and Its Consequences
9.2 Balancing Economic Growth and Environmental Preservation
9.3 Community Conflicts and Tourism
9.4 The Future of Tourism: Virtual Tourism and Beyond

Chapter 10: The Future of Tourist Dollars
10.1 Emerging Trends in Tourism
10.2 Technology's Impact on Tourism
10.3 Strategies for Sustainable and Inclusive Tourism
10.4 Preparing Local Economies for the Future

INTRODUCTION

The 21st century has witnessed a spike in international tourism on a scale that has never been seen before, with an ever-increasing number of people traveling to different parts of the world in search of fresh experiences, cultures, and landscapes. This boom has not only contributed to the development of an industry that possesses tremendous economic significance, but it has also significantly transformed the dynamics of local economies all over the world. The transformative potential of tourism as a driver of economic growth and development is becoming more and more apparent. The money that tourists spend in local communities is the vital force that revitalizes and maintains those communities. Tourist dollars serve as the lifeblood.

The phenomena of tourist dollars supporting growth in local economies has exceeded the realm

of ordinary financial transactions and has emerged as a force that alters the fabric of society. This force influences a variety of aspects, including the development of small businesses, infrastructure, and the preservation of cultural traditions, amongst other things. To get a full picture of this multidimensional influence, you need to conduct a sophisticated investigation that delves into the complex dynamic that exists between the international tourism industry and the communities that it affects.

This all-encompassing investigation aims to decipher the complexity of the symbiotic relationship that exists between tourism and local economies, putting light on both the benefits and the challenges that are brought about by the dynamic interdependence that exists between these two spheres of influence. We hope to provide a thorough knowledge of the larger ramifications and far-reaching repercussions of this economic phenomenon by investigating the numerous ways in which tourist money permeate and affect local communities. This will allow us to present a more accurate picture of the scope of these effects.

The first chapter of this exposition lays the basis by establishing a crystal clear definition of tourism and outlining the primary components of an economy that relies heavily on tourism. In addition to this, it digs into the several economic models and frameworks that are the basis for the functioning of this sector. This chapter lays the groundwork for the forthcoming investigation of the significant influence that tourism has on the economics of local communities by providing an explanation of the industry's intricate workings.

Chapter 2, which builds upon the framework laid in the previous chapter, examines the effects of tourism on a more local level. In this article, we investigate the ways in which tourist dollars enter the economic environment of local communities and analyze the role that these dollars play in the creation of employment possibilities, the expansion of infrastructure, and general economic prosperity.

This chapter tries to provide a thorough understanding of the real-world ramifications of this global sector by illustrating, through in-depth case studies, the tangible effects of tourism on the socio-economic landscape of individual locations. These repercussions can be seen as having a direct bearing on the tourism industry.

In Chapter 3, the attention changes to the significant part that is performed by small enterprises within the setting of economies that are driven by tourism. We dive into the various ways in which these businesses contribute to and benefit from the influx of tourist dollars by highlighting the vital role that small businesses play within these regional economies. In addition, this chapter emphasizes the significance of putting appropriate support systems in place to promote the growth and long-term sustainability of essential economic contributors such as tourism and agriculture.

Within the context of modern tourism, sustainability stands out as an extremely important factor to take into account. The purpose of this chapter is to provide an explanation of the idea of sustainable tourism as well as its consequences for the local economies that it has an effect on and the surrounding environment. This chapter aims to emphasize the need of striking a delicate balance between economic growth and environmental conservation within the setting of the tourist economy by analyzing the evolving trends and practices that promote responsible and sustainable tourism. This will be done by studying the evolving trends and practices that promote responsible and sustainable tourism.

The protection of cultural heritage is an additional essential facet that the tourism industry must address. The fifth chapter dives into the complex relationship that exists between tourism and cultural heritage, illuminating the ways in which tourism can either aid in the preservation of local cultural identities or, on the other hand, constitute a threat to such identities' inherent integrity. This chapter seeks to shed light on the ways in which local communities can leverage their cultural assets to stimulate economic growth while simultaneously protecting their distinctive cultural heritage. This will be accomplished by exploring a variety of strategies and practices that make it possible for cultural preservation and tourism to coexist in a way that is mutually beneficial.

The creation of necessary infrastructure is an essential precondition for the continued expansion of economies that are dependent on tourism. In Chapter 6, we look into the essential role that infrastructure plays in both facilitating and accommodating the influx of tourists. This covers a wide range of topics, from public services and amenities to transit networks and hotels.This chapter offers insights into the mechanisms through which effective infrastructure planning and investment can spur economic development and ensure the sustainability of tourist-driven regions by analyzing the symbiotic relationship between the development of infrastructure and the growth of local economies. Specifically, the chapter examines the relationship between the growth of local economies and the development of infrastructure.

Marketing and promotion are vital instruments for luring and maintaining tourist traffic in local economies, hence it is important to focus on both of these areas. The tourist business is examined in great detail in Chapter 7, which focuses on the many different marketing tactics and initiatives that are now in use. This chapter highlights the value of targeted and strategic promotional activities in supporting sustained economic growth within local communities by analyzing the role that successful marketing plays in stimulating visitor interest. It does so by examining the role that effective marketing plays in stimulating tourist interest.

The direction that the tourism industry will head in is heavily influenced by the policies and
regulatory frameworks that are put in place by the government. The topic of regulatory monitoring, policy formulation, and the establishment of tourism promotion agencies is the focus of discussion in Chapter 8. This chapter is entirely devoted to examining the diverse influence of government interventions. This chapter seeks to highlight the crucial significance of establishing an enabling environment that is favorable to sustainable and equitable economic growth by studying the ways in which governmental activities can either promote or impede the growth of tourism-dependent local economies. It does so by evaluating the ways in which these actions can be either positive or negative.

However, this mutually beneficial link between tourism and the economics of local communities is not without its share of difficulties and debates. The complicated problems that arise as a result of this context are discussed in Chapter 9. These problems include the negative effects of overtourism, disputes that arise within local communities, and the potential ramifications of emerging trends in virtual tourism. This chapter intends to inspire critical reflections on the future trajectory of tourism and local economic development by acknowledging and addressing these issues. It also places an emphasis on the necessity of adopting methods that are both sustainable and inclusive in order to minimize the negative consequences that are caused by these challenges.

In Chapter 10, we take a forward-looking look at the future trajectory of tourist dollars within local economies, which gives an interesting assessment of this topic. This chapter provides a glimpse of the prospective growth of the tourism sector by extrapolating emerging trends and technology advancements. The information in this chapter was gathered from previous research. In addition, it underlines the necessity for regional economies to implement proactive policies that can adapt these changes and assure their sustained growth and resilience in the face of an ever-evolving global tourist scene. These methods may be found here.

1. **The Importance of Tourism**

The phenomena of tourism is a global phenomenon that has far-reaching repercussions that go far beyond the realm of travel and pleasure. It helps to stimulate cultural exchange as well as economic growth and international cooperation, all of which are essential to the functioning of the global economy. It is impossible to overestimate the significance of tourism since it has such a profound impact on so many facets of our lives, economy, and civilizations.

The expansion of the economy and the creation of new jobs

One of the most important contributions made by tourism is the function it plays in fostering economic expansion and the creation of new jobs. Every year, the tourist industry is responsible for bringing in billions of dollars in revenue, making it a significant contributor to the economy. It is the primary source of income for millions of people all over the world, including those working in hotels and restaurants, as well as those providing transportation services and guiding tourists. Tourism is a substantial contribution to the Gross Domestic Product (GDP) and a primary source of foreign currency for a great number of nations. When tourists visit a location, they spend money on things like lodging, food, shopping, and numerous attractions. This spending puts money into the hands of local businesses and helps the local economy. The repercussions of a change in one area of the economy can be felt in many other areas as well, such as agriculture, construction, and transportation.

Exchange of cultures and mutual comprehension

Travel and tourism have an important role in the dissemination of culture and the promotion of international understanding. It gives tourists the opportunity to completely submerge themselves in unfamiliar cultures, customs, and ways of life, which helps cultivate a sense of empathy, tolerance, and appreciation for diversity. Tourists are afforded the opportunity to interact with the communities in which they are vacationing, to take part in cultural celebrations, and to try regional foods. Tourists are able to get insights into the lives of the people they come into contact with through these experiences, and in turn, they are able to share their own cultures with the locations they visit. This sharing of thoughts and experiences contributes to the dismantling of preconceived notions and the construction of communication bridges between various nations and cultures.

The Safekeeping of Our Cultural Traditions

The protection of cultural assets is frequently dependent on the contributions made by the tourism industry. The continued operation of a great number of traditional customs, historical places, and museums as well as the cash generated by tourists is essential to their survival. When travelers pay a visit to these cultural landmarks, they are helping to ensure that these priceless artifacts will be around for future generations to enjoy. The money that is made from tourism can be used to pay for the preservation of endangered languages and cultures, the digitization of old texts and artifacts, and the upkeep and repair of historical landmarks.

In its most basic form, tourism serves as an incentive for local communities to take care of and exhibit their cultural traditions.

Protection of the Natural Environment

When handled correctly, tourism has the potential to be a driving force in the protection of natural resources, despite the fact that it may at times create environmental problems. It is common for natural wonders, national parks, and animal reserves to rely on tourism as their primary source of revenue in order to pay their protection and conservation activities. Programs that maintain ecosystems, protect endangered species, and promote sustainable resource management can be funded by entrance fees, contributions, and sustainable tourism practices, among other avenues. In addition, responsible tourism has the potential to increase knowledge about environmental issues and motivate passengers to be more sensitive of the influence they have on the environment.

The Development of Infrastructure

Places that are open to tourists often see rapid growth in their infrastructure as a direct result of the influx of tourists. Investing in infrastructure could be motivated by the fact that the tourism industry requires services like lodging, transportation, and amenities. In order to meet the requirements of the tourism business, renovations and expansions are frequently made to areas such as airports, highways, hotels, and public facilities. Not only are tourists going to gain from this, but the locals are going to see an overall improvement in their quality of life as well.

The Promotion of Regional Growth and Inclusivity

Tourism has the potential to promote regional development and inclusivity by distributing economic advantages to places that may otherwise struggle. This can be done by bringing tourists to locations that would otherwise be underserved. Smaller communities and rural places have the potential to benefit greatly from tourism, despite the fact that most people's attention is focused on larger cities and popular tourist destinations. It is possible for tourists to deviate from well-trodden paths in order to discover lesser-known destinations, which contributes to a more equitable distribution of revenue. In addition, local entrepreneurs and small enterprises in rural and distant locations frequently discover opportunities to survive by catering to tourists, which contributes to the diversification of the local economy.

Relations with Other Countries and World Peace

The development of tourism has the ability to contribute to international amity and collaboration. People from various nations develop deeper personal relationships with one another as well as a more in-depth awareness of the cultures and points of view of the other nations through travel and interaction. These relationships have the potential to serve as a cornerstone for the practice of diplomacy and the maintenance of peaceful relations between nations.

Furthermore, governments that rely on tourism earnings have a vested interest in maintaining political stability and security because these characteristics directly effect the attractiveness of their countries as tourist destinations. This is because these factors directly impact their attractiveness as tourist destinations.

Education and Intellectual Acquiring

The education that may be gained from travel is second to none. Travel and tourism offer several chances for individual development and education that go well beyond the confines of the traditional classroom setting. When people travel, they are exposed to different surroundings, cultures, and languages, which broadens their horizons and increases their knowledge. Being exposed to a wide variety of cultures and histories piques one's intellectual curiosity and has the potential to kindle a love of learning and discovery that lasts a lifetime. The educational value of tourism has been recognized by a wide variety of educational institutions and organizations, which has led to the proliferation of programs and scholarships designed to encourage and facilitate international cultural exchange.

A Good State of Health and Well-Being

Travel and tourism have the potential to have a beneficial impact on both health and well-being. People are able to take a break from the mundane and stressful aspects of daily life, relax, and refuel their batteries when they travel. The mental and physical health of an individual can be improved by participating in a variety of activities, surroundings, and eating styles. In addition, the experiences that one has when traveling frequently generate lifelong memories and strengthen ties with loved ones, both of which contribute to emotional health and happiness.

Encouragement of Creative Activity and the Arts

Travel and tourism have the potential to inspire new forms of expression and creativity. In order to attract tourists, several locations have developed their very own distinctive cultural manifestations. These creative efforts may take the form of music, dancing, written or visual arts, or any combination of these. In addition, the presence of tourists can serve as a catalyst for the development of the local creative community, which can result in the opening of art galleries, theaters, and other cultural establishments.

Connection with Other People and Empathy

Because it brings people from all different walks of life together, tourism is a powerful force in the cultivation of human connection and empathy. Travelers get the opportunity to engage in conversation with residents of the area and gain insight into the joys and struggles of daily life there. These encounters frequently result in the growth of empathy, comprehension, and a perception of a humanity that is shared by all parties involved. When people go on vacation, they usually gain a newfound

awareness for the global community as well as a determination to work toward making the world a better place.
Diversification of the Economic System
Communities' reliance on a single industry can be reduced, and economic diversity can be increased, through the growth of the tourism industry. The adoption of tourism in regions that have historically relied on agriculture or manufacturing can result in a significant boost to the local economy in those regions. Diversification of the economy can improve a country's capacity for resilience and stability, particularly in the face of economic downturns in other industries.

1. **Defining Tourism**

   The tourism business is both diverse and dynamic, and it has seen substantial change over the course of its existence. Because it covers such a broad spectrum of pursuits and encounters, tourism is not as easy to pin down as its definition might lead one to believe it is. The most fundamental aspect of tourism is the act of moving people from one location to another for a variety of reasons, including commerce, pleasure, and the exploration of different cultures. When attempting to grasp the full meaning of tourism, it is necessary to take into account the many facets it possesses as well as the effects it has on people's lives, communities, and economies.

   The act of traveling for the purpose of amusement, leisure, or the quest of new experiences is one definition of tourism at its most fundamental level. People go on vacation to get away from their normal routines and become used to new situations. These people travel both near and far to reach their destinations. These trips may take the form of vacations to well-known tourist hotspots, weekend excursions to secluded retreats, or travels to far-flung lands in search of unfamiliar cultural practices and customs. The tourist industry provides a wide variety of opportunities for leisure and relaxation, such as sunbathing on a beach that has been kissed by the sun, trekking through isolated mountain routes, or seeing historical places.

   However, tourism is not restricted just to people traveling for pleasure. A substantial part of the market is comprised of business tourism, sometimes known as corporate travel and sometimes referred to as simply business travel. People that travel for business-related reasons, such as to attend conferences, meetings, trade exhibitions, and other industry events are participating in this subset of tourism. Business tourism makes a significant contribution to the overall economy by bolstering sectors such as the lodging industry, the transportation sector, and the event management sector.

   Cultural tourism is an additional important facet of the tourism industry. The investigation of a culture's historical and artistic landmarks, as well as its customs and practices, is the primary focus of cultural tourism. Activities such as going to museums, art galleries, archaeological sites, and cultural festivals are some of the things that tourists do in order to obtain an understanding of the history and traditions of a specific region.

This type of tourism is not only about going to see the sites; rather, it focuses on learning about and enjoying the cultural diversity of the place you are visiting.

A further component of the sector is known as adventure tourism. Adventure travelers are looking for activities that will get their hearts racing, such as rock climbing, white water rafting, trekking, and safaris. They are drawn to locations that offer activities that are both exciting and physically taxing on the body. People that desire excitement and are prepared to move outside of their comfort zones in order to discover the natural environment are the target demographic for the field of adventure tourism.

The reasons people travel have also changed in tandem with the development of tourism. In response to a growing concern for the protection of environmental and cultural resources, the tourism industries of ecotourism and sustainable tourism have evolved. Ecotourism is a form of responsible travel to natural regions that aims to minimize a visitor's harmful impact on the surrounding environment. This kind of tourism frequently contributes to conservation efforts, teaches visitors about the ecosystems of the area they are visiting, and encourages the use of sustainable practices. On the other side, sustainable tourism is one that aims to reduce the amount of damage that is done to the environment, as well as the economy and the communities that are visited. Both ecotourism and sustainable tourism have the same overall goal, which is to strike a balance between the positive aspects of travel and the imperative to conserve and maintain our planet.

2. **Tourism's Global Impact**

The leisure and travel sectors of tourism are only a small part of the enormous global tourism industry's overall impact. It exerts a major influence on the economy, acts as a facilitator for the transmission of cultural ideas, contributes significantly to the expansion of physical infrastructure, and plays a key role in international relations. The effects of tourism can be felt all over the world and have a significant influence on the course of history in a variety of countries and localities.

1. **Stimulating Economic Growth:** The ability of tourism to stimulate economic growth is one of the most obvious and significant effects of the industry. The tourism business is responsible for an enormous infusion of capital, the generation of new job openings, the stimulation of new investment, and a contribution to the gross domestic product. This economic expansion has an effect

not only on major tourist attractions but also on periphery regions and tiny towns that are financially dependent on tourism.
2. **The provision of work opportunities:** the tourism industry is a big contributor to worldwide employment. It offers employment opportunities to people from a wide range of backgrounds, including as hotel workers, tour guides, restaurant employees, transportation workers, and artisans. The tourist industry provides chances for individuals to make a living and generate income, making it an effective tool in the fight against unemployment and underemployment. These opportunities can be found anywhere from densely populated urban regions to distant rural enclaves.
3. The Development of Infrastructure The desire to accommodate and provide services to tourists is frequently what drives investments in infrastructure. In order to satisfy the requirements of the tourism business, airports, highways, hotels, restaurants, and public amenities are undergoing renovations and expansions. This not only improves the experience that tourists have, but it also raises the general quality of life for local inhabitants, who get the benefits of better transportation and services as a result of this development.
4. Cultural Exchange Because it brings together people from all over the world, tourism plays an important role in fostering cultural exchange and mutual understanding. Travelers cultivate qualities such as empathy, tolerance, and appreciation for variety by fully submerging themselves in the cultures, customs, and traditions of the places they visit. It is possible for tourists to engage in conversation with residents of the area, take part in cultural activities, and try regional food, all of which contribute to the formation of personal connections that are not constrained by borders and help to develop goodwill across nations.
5. The Protection of Cultural Heritage The upkeep of a lot of historical locations, museums, and cultural traditions is dependent on the money that is made from tourists visiting those locations. When tourists pay a visit to these cultural attractions, they make a contribution toward the preservation and restoration of heritage sites. This helps to ensure that these places will be around for decades to come. Communities can receive a financial boost from tourism, which can serve as an incentive for them to preserve their cultural assets.
6. Environmental Conservation Despite the fact that tourism can have adverse effects on the surrounding environment, if it is carefully managed, it also has the potential to be a driving force in the fight to preserve the natural world. It is common practice for natural marvels, national parks, and animal reserves to rely on funds generated by tourism to finance their ongoing conservation efforts. Programs that safeguard ecosystems, endangered animals, and natural resources are funded by entrance fees, contributions, and sustainable tourist practices.

7. Tourism's Positive Effects on World Peace and Cooperation Tourism is a force for good in international relations. The personal relationships and cultural knowledge that are developed as a result of travel can serve as a basis for diplomacy and harmonious relations between nations. People-to-people connections are generated when two individuals meet each other for the first time. In addition, nations whose economies are dependent on tourism have a vested interest in preserving political stability and security in order to entice tourists to visit their countries.
8. The Possibilities for Education Traveling provides opportunities for education that are priceless. Travel broadens people's horizons and deepens their understanding of the world by introducing them to different cultures, histories, and geographical regions. Educational establishments and organizations acknowledge the significance of tourism as a tool for learning, and as a result, they frequently provide funding opportunities in the form of grants and scholarships to encourage cultural exchange and travel.
9. Regional Development and Inclusivity Tourism encourages regional development and inclusivity by transferring economic benefits to communities that may otherwise struggle to survive on their own. Smaller villages, more isolated locations, and rural areas all have the potential to benefit from tourism if they can offer experiences that are distinctive and genuine. The gaps that exist between urban and rural areas can be reduced by diversifying the economy and increasing income, which both contribute to a society that is more egalitarian.

B. Purpose and Scope of the Book

"Tourist Dollars Fueling Growth in Local Economies" aims to provide a comprehensive understanding of how the influx of tourist dollars shapes communities, industries, and the overall socio-economic landscape by conducting an in-depth investigation of the complex relationship that exists between tourism and local economies. This will be accomplished by providing an exhaustive look at how tourist dollars shape communities, industries, and the overall socio-economic landscape. This book aims to shed light on the myriad of affects that tourism has, ranging from the growth of the economy and the preservation of cultural traditions to the preservation of the environment and the issues posed by overtourism. The reader will be able to comprehend the immense significance of tourism and its far-reaching impacts after reading this book because its goal and scope are to educate and motivate them.

1. **An Exposition of the Concept of Tourism and Its Significance:**
   The first section of the book is devoted to a comprehensive analysis of the meaning behind the
   term "tourism." It offers a definition of tourism as well as a breakdown of its several subcategories, including cultural tourism, business tourism, adventure

tourism, and leisure tourism. The objective of this section is to provide the groundwork for a more in-depth study of the topic at hand.

2. **Effects on the Economy of the Local Area:**
In the second chapter, we examine the economic effects of tourism on a more regional scale. This article investigates the ways in which revenue from tourists permeates the economic ecosystem of local communities. This chapter provides a clear view of the real-world ramifications of this worldwide sector by illustrating, through thorough case studies, the concrete effects that tourism has on the socio-economic landscape of individual locations. This chapter focuses on tourism as a global enterprise.

3. **The Role of Small Businesses and What They Do:**
In Chapter 3, the attention changes to the significant part that is performed by small enterprises within the setting of economies that are driven by tourism. This chapter discusses the importance of assisting locally owned firms and provides instances of how such companies have contributed to the expansion of the economy in the real world.

4. **Tourism that is sustainable**
In Chapter 4, the topic of sustainable tourism gets the spotlight. Within the framework of the tourism industry, this chapter emphasizes the significance of environmentally conscious vacationing and the necessity of striking a delicate balance between expanding the economy and preserving the natural world. Case examples and recommendations for best practices in sustainable tourism are included.

5. **The protection of cultural heritage:**
The delicate relationship that exists between tourism and cultural heritage is investigated in Chapter 5. It places a strong emphasis on the preservation and promotion of local cultures, demonstrating how tourism can both fuel economic growth and conserve unique cultural identities at the same time.

6. **The Development of Physical Infrastructure:**
In Chapter 6, we discuss the critical function that infrastructure plays in the process of hosting tourists. This chapter demonstrates how key factors such as transportation, hotels, and public services all play a role in propelling economic expansion. Through the presentation of a variety of case studies, it demonstrates the positive effect that investments in infrastructure may have on local economies.

7. **Advertising and Public Relations:**
The importance of marketing and promotion in the process of drawing in tourists is examined in depth in Chapter 7.
The reader will come away with a better understanding of the significance of public-private partnerships in the field of tourist promotion as well as the

myriad of marketing tactics, both online and offline. Case studies are illustrative examples of efficient methods of marketing.

8. **An Overview of the Functions of Government:**
   In the eighth chapter, we investigate the critical part that governments play in determining the course that the tourism industry will take. Within the context of tourism, it discusses governmental policies, regulatory frameworks, oversight mechanisms, tourism promotion agencies, and taxation.

9. **Difficulties and Debates Concerning:**
   However, this mutually beneficial link between tourism and the economics of local communities is not without its share of difficulties and debates. The complicated problems that arise are discussed in Chapter 9. These problems include overtourism, conflicts between communities, and the potential impact of developing trends in virtual tourism. This chapter intends to prompt critical observations on the future trajectory of tourism and local economic development by first identifying and then addressing the problems that are presented in this section.

10. **The Prospects for the Money Generated by Tourists:**

The last chapter provides the reader with a glimpse into the potential role that tourist monies will play in local economies. This chapter provides a glimpse of the prospective growth of the tourism sector by extrapolating emerging trends and technology advancements. The information in this chapter was gathered from previous research. In addition, it underlines the necessity for regional economies to implement proactive policies that can adapt these changes and assure their sustained growth and resilience in the face of an ever-evolving global tourist scene. These methods may be found here.

The final chapter of the book provides a summary of the most important aspects and emphasizes the continual evolution of tourism. It concludes by providing some closing remarks on the significant role that tourism plays in fostering local economic growth and highlighting the importance of responsible and environmentally friendly tourism practices.

This book has an expansive scope, with the goal of covering a wide variety of subjects relating to tourism and the influence that it has on the economies of various localities. The reader will get a complete understanding of the ways in which the spending of tourist money influences and transforms communities all over the world through the use of case studies, best practices, and analyses that provoke thought. This book provides readers with the knowledge and insights necessary to successfully navigate the ever-changing world of tourism, hence supporting sustainable growth and prosperity in their particular communities.

This is accomplished by providing a methodical investigation of five essential facets of tourism. In the end, the goal of this book is to build a better awareness among readers for the transformative impact that tourism can have on local economies by enlightening and inspiring them.

C. Overview of Chapters

The book "Tourist Dollars Fueling Growth in Local Economies" is an in-depth investigation into the significant influence that tourism has on regional economies. A well-organized and informative journey through the intricate web of economic linkages, cultural preservation, infrastructure development, marketing techniques, and government legislation that characterize the tourism sector is provided by the book's ten chapters. This summary acts as a guide to the individual chapters, highlighting the most important ideas and goals that are discussed in each one.

Understanding the Tourism Industry is Covered in Chapter 1.

By providing a definition of tourism and investigating its relevance on a worldwide scale, this introductory chapter establishes the groundwork for the rest of the book. It presents fundamental ideas related to the tourism industry, such as economic models, and describes the fundamental components of the tourist economy. The purpose of this article is to present the reader with a foundational understanding of tourism and the myriad of impacts that it has.

The Local Economic Impact is the topic of Chapter 2.

In the second chapter, we delve further into the economic effects that tourism has on the surrounding community. It demonstrates how the revenue generated by tourism permeates the economic landscape of local communities, which in turn influences employment, the development of infrastructure, and economic growth. Case studies are used throughout this chapter to provide real-world insights into the concrete consequences that tourism may have on particular locations.

Tourism and the Role of Small Businesses in Chapter 3.

This chapter places an emphasis on the significance of small enterprises, which play an essential part in economies that are driven by tourism. The reader will gain an understanding of the vital role that small businesses play in the tourism industry as well as the necessary support structures for their expansion. The importance of small enterprises to the growth of the local economy is illustrated through a discussion of both their achievements and the obstacles they must overcome.

Tourism That Is Sustainable, Chapter 4.

The need of environmentally conscious vacationing is emphasized throughout Chapter 4. This chapter provides an introduction to the ideas of sustainable tourism and emphasizes how important it is to strike a balance between economic expansion and the preservation of the natural environment. It highlights the vital need for responsible travel practices by showcasing real-world instances of sustainable tourism and the best practices currently in use in the industry.

Tourism and the Protection of Cultural Heritage (Chapter 5).

The interaction between tourism and the preservation of cultural traditions is the topic of the fifth chapter. Within the framework of tourism, it investigates the significance of cultural attractions as well as the preservation and dissemination of native cultures. This chapter explains how tourism can contribute to the preservation of cultural traditions while also supporting economic growth through the use of specific instances.

Infrastructure growth and tourism are the topics of Chapter 6.

In Chapter 6, we look at how critically important infrastructure is to the tourism industry. This chapter focuses on how investments in infrastructure can fuel economic development and highlights the importance of transportation, lodging, and public services for hosting tourists. Case studies based on the real world provide valuable insight into the effects that the development of infrastructure has on local economies.

The Marketing and Promotion Chapter (Chapter 7).

The concepts of marketing and promotion in the tourism industry are discussed in depth in Chapter 7. This article investigates the impact that efficient marketing methods play in recruiting tourists and connecting with the general public. The necessity of public-private partnerships in the promotion of tourism is stressed, and both online and offline marketing tactics are examined. Case studies are used as concrete illustrations of successful approaches to marketing techniques.

The Function of the Government is Discussed in Chapter 8.

The tourist business is subject to a variety of governmental laws and regulations, the discussion of which is the primary topic of Chapter 8 of this book. This chapter covers topics such as legislation, oversight, tourism marketing agencies, and taxation as it relates to the chapter's main topic, which is the role that the government plays in defining the trajectory of the tourist industry. This chapter offers insights into the implications on local economies by exploring the interaction between government policies and tourism. Specifically, it looks at how the two are intertwined.

The Challenging Debates and Contentious Issues of Chapter 9.

The connection between tourism and regional economies is not without its share of difficulties and debates, all of which are discussed in Chapter 9 of this book. We look at both the causes and effects of excessive tourism, as well as the imperative of striking a healthy balance between economic expansion and environmental protection. In addition to this, the chapter explores the tensions that might arise within communities as a result of tourism and analyzes the potential future of tourism, including the concept of virtual tourism. It stimulates critical observations on the future of tourism and the influence that tourism will have on the economics of local communities.

The future of revenue from tourists is discussed in Chapter 10.

The tenth and last chapter offers a look into the potential impact that tourism spending will have on local economies in the future. Topics covered include emerging trends in tourism, the role of technology, and methods for inclusive and sustainable tourism. This chapter places an emphasis on the necessity for local economies to get ready for the changing environment of tourism in order to ensure their continuing growth and resilience in the face of adversity.

Chapter 1

Understanding the Tourist Economy

The global tourist economy is a complicated and multi-layered structure that includes a diverse assortment of businesses and fields of endeavor all over the world. Travel refers to the act of moving from one location to another for a variety of reasons, including business, pleasure, or the discovery of different cultures. To gain an understanding of the tourism economy, it is necessary to investigate its fundamental aspects, as well as its relevance on a worldwide scale and its significant influence on the economies of local communities and regional areas. In the course of this in-depth conversation, we are going to delve into the intricate particulars of the tourism industry, investigating its many facets as well as the primary elements that influence it.

1. **An Overview of Tourism**
   Tourism can be broken down into its component parts, the most fundamental of which is the act of traveling for the purpose of amusement, leisure, or the quest of new experiences. People go on vacation to get away from their normal routines and become used to new situations. These people travel both near and far

to reach their destinations. These trips may take the form of vacations to well-known tourist hotspots, weekend excursions to secluded retreats, or travels to far-flung lands in search of unfamiliar cultural practices and customs. The tourist industry provides a wide variety of opportunities for leisure and relaxation, such as sunbathing on a beach that has been kissed by the sun, trekking through isolated mountain routes, or seeing historical places.

However, tourism is not restricted just to people traveling for pleasure. A substantial part of the market is comprised of business tourism, sometimes known as corporate travel and sometimes referred to as simply business travel. People that travel for business-related reasons, such as to attend conferences, meetings, trade exhibitions, and other industry events are participating in this subset of tourism. Business tourism makes a significant contribution to the overall economy by bolstering sectors such as the lodging industry, the transportation sector, and the event management sector.

Cultural tourism is an additional important facet of the tourism industry. The investigation of a culture's historical and artistic landmarks, as well as its customs and practices, is the primary focus of cultural tourism.

Activities such as going to museums, art galleries, archaeological sites, and cultural festivals are some of the things that tourists do in order to obtain an understanding of the history and traditions of a specific region. This type of tourism is not only about going to see the sites; rather, it focuses on learning about and enjoying the cultural diversity of the place you are visiting.

A further component of the sector is known as adventure tourism. Adventure travelers are looking for activities that will get their hearts racing, such as rock climbing, white water rafting, trekking, and safaris. They are drawn to locations that offer activities that are both exciting and physically taxing on the body. People that desire excitement and are prepared to move outside of their comfort zones in order to discover the natural environment are the target demographic for the field of adventure tourism.

On the other side, cruise tourism entails tourists visiting various locations while sailing onboard a cruise ship. These tourists are able to visit a variety of destinations and engage with the local culture without being need to frequently alter their lodging arrangements.

Tourism is, at its core, a complex and multidimensional industry that comprises a broad range of activities, reasons for traveling, and experiences had by travelers. It is crucial to acknowledge its many facets and its importance in the economy of the entire world, despite the fact that it is commonly connected with things like leisure and entertainment.

2. **The Significance of Tourism on a Global Scale**

The contributions that the tourism industry makes to a variety of facets of society as well as the economy give it a huge global significance. Let's investigate some of the primary reasons why tourism is such an important part of the economy of the entire world.

Impact on the Economy: Tourism has a significant positive impact on economic growth and the generation of jobs. It results in annual revenue of multiple billions of dollars and creates employment opportunities for tens of millions of people all over the world. Tourism is a significant contribution to the Gross Domestic Product (GDP) and a significant source of foreign currency revenues in many nations. The revenue that is generated by tourism is not restricted to a single industry but rather extends to a variety of different fields, such as the hospitality industry, the transportation industry, the food and beverage services industry, and the entertainment industry.

The tourism industry is a big contributor to employment opportunities all over the world. It offers employment opportunities to people from a wide range of backgrounds, including as hotel workers, tour guides, restaurant employees, transportation workers, and artisans.

The tourist industry provides chances for individuals to make a living and generate income, making it an effective tool in the fight against unemployment and underemployment. These opportunities can be found anywhere from densely populated urban regions to distant rural enclaves.

Investment in Infrastructure: The requirement to accommodate and provide for the needs of tourists is often what motivates these types of investments. In order to satisfy the requirements of the tourism business, airports, highways, hotels, restaurants, and public amenities are undergoing renovations and expansions. This not only improves the experience that tourists have, but it also raises the general quality of life for local inhabitants, who get the benefits of better transportation and services as a result of this development.

Exchange of Cultures: Tourism acts as a conduit for the exchange of cultures and promotes mutual understanding between different peoples and nations. It gives tourists the opportunity to completely submerge themselves in unfamiliar cultures, customs, and ways of life, which helps cultivate a sense of empathy, tolerance, and appreciation for diversity. Tourists are afforded the opportunity to interact with the communities in which they are vacationing, to take part in cultural celebrations, and to try regional foods. Tourists are able to get insights into the lives of the people they come into contact with through these experiences, and in turn, they are able to share their own cultures with the locations they visit. This sharing of thoughts and experiences contributes to the dismantling of preconceived notions and the construction of communication bridges between various nations and cultures.

The preservation of cultural heritage relies heavily on the income brought in by tourism, as a great number of historical sites, museums, and traditional customs rely on this income to continue operating. When travelers pay a visit to these cultural landmarks, they are helping to ensure that these priceless artifacts will be around for future generations to enjoy. The money that is made from tourism can be used to pay for the preservation of endangered languages and cultures, the digitization of old texts and artifacts, and the upkeep and repair of historical landmarks. At its core, tourism serves as an incentive for local communities to value and exhibit the cultural resources that are unique to them.

Environmental Conservation Despite the fact that tourism can result in negative environmental impacts if it is not appropriately managed, it also has the potential to be a driving force in environmental conservation. It is common for natural wonders, national parks, and animal reserves to rely on tourism as their primary source of revenue in order to pay their protection and conservation activities.

Programs that maintain ecosystems, protect endangered species, and promote sustainable resource management can be funded by entrance fees, contributions, and sustainable tourism practices, among other avenues. In addition, responsible tourism has the potential to increase knowledge about environmental issues and motivate passengers to be more sensitive of the influence they have on the environment.

Tourism and International Relations: Tourism has the potential to be a unifying force that helps nations work together and promotes peace in the world. People from various nations develop deeper personal relationships with one another as well as a more in-depth awareness of the cultures and points of view of the other nations through travel and interaction. These relationships have the potential to serve as a cornerstone for the practice of diplomacy and the maintenance of peaceful relations between nations. Furthermore, governments that rely on tourism earnings have a vested interest in maintaining political stability and security because these characteristics directly effect the attractiveness of their countries as tourist destinations. This is because these factors directly impact their attractiveness as tourist destinations.

Education and learning: Traveling provides an educational experience that is unparalleled in its value. Travel and tourism offer several chances for individual development and education that go well beyond the confines of the traditional classroom setting. When people travel, they are exposed to different surroundings, cultures, and languages, which broadens their horizons and increases their knowledge. Being exposed to a wide variety of cultures and histories piques one's intellectual curiosity and has the potential to kindle a love of learning and discovery that lasts a lifetime. The educational value of tourism has been recognized by a wide variety of educational institutions and organizations, which has led to the proliferation of programs and scholarships designed to encourage and facilitate international cultural exchange.

Tourism has the potential to have a beneficial impact on both a person's health and their overall well-being. People are able to take a break from the mundane and stressful aspects of daily life, relax, and refuel their batteries when they travel. The mental and physical health of an individual can be improved by participating in a variety of activities, surroundings, and eating styles. In addition, the experiences that one has when traveling frequently generate lifelong memories and strengthen ties with loved ones, both of which contribute to emotional health and happiness.

Tourism has the potential to serve as a driving force in the advancement of artistic expression and creative endeavors. In order to attract tourists, several locations have developed their very own distinctive cultural manifestations. These creative efforts may take the form of music, dancing, written or visual arts, or any combination of these. In addition, the presence of tourists can serve as a catalyst for the development of the local creative community, which can result in the opening of art galleries, theaters, and other cultural establishments.

Human Connection and Empathy Human connection and empathy are fostered by tourism since it brings together people whose origins are very different from one another. Travelers get the opportunity to engage in conversation with residents of the area and gain insight into the joys and struggles of daily life there. These encounters frequently result in the growth of empathy, comprehension, and a perception of a humanity that is shared by all parties involved. When people go on vacation, they usually gain a newfound awareness for the global community as well as a determination to work toward making the world a better place.

Diversification of the Economy Tourism has the potential to lessen a community's reliance on a single industry while also adding to the economy's capacity for diversification. The adoption of tourism in regions that have historically relied on agriculture or manufacturing can result in a significant boost to the local economy in those regions. Diversification of the economy can improve a country's capacity for resilience and stability, particularly in the face of economic downturns in other industries.

1.1 The Tourist Economy Defined

The travel industry, which is also often known as the tourist economy, is a system that is intricate and multi-faceted, and it has an international scope. It comprises a wide variety of activities and services that cater to the requirements and wishes of visitors, whether they are looking for opportunity to relax, engage in exciting activities, experience different cultures, or further their professional careers. The economy of tourism plays an essential part in local, regional, and global contexts, and it has significant implications for the economy, culture, and the environment.

Determining What the Tourism Industry Is:

At its core, the tourist economy consists of a wide and linked web of economic activities and services that are centered on travel and tourism. It includes a wide variety of stakeholders, such as visitors, enterprises, governments, and communities in the area, all of which play an essential role in ensuring its successful operation. Within the confines of this concept, we are able to analyze the myriad aspects and constituents that come together to form the tourism economy.

Individuals that travel for a variety of reasons make up the bulk of tourists, who are the driving force behind the tourism industry. Travelers who are there for business or pleasure, those who are interested in culture or in seeking out new experiences are all examples of tourists. They are the primary force behind the demand for tourism-related services and activities, which in turn drives the industry as a whole.

Services and Activities in the Tourism Industry The tourism industry is made up of a vast variety of services and activities that are geared toward satisfying the requirements and whims of vacationers. These can include things like lodging, means of transportation, food and drink, entertainment, cultural encounters, excursion excursions, and a whole host of other possibilities. These services are offered by a wide variety of companies, some of which are hotels, airlines, restaurants, tour operators, and others.

Infrastructure Relating to Tourism: In order to manage the flood of tourists, regions frequently make investments in infrastructure that is related to tourism. This includes airports, highways, hotels, resorts, attractions, and other amenities that make the trip more enjoyable for tourists.

Towns Nearby: The travel and tourism industry is intricately entwined with the towns near its destinations and the people who live there. Tourism has the potential to foster economic expansion, generate new employment possibilities, and supply a source of revenue for existing local businesses. However, it may also provide issues to local communities in terms of the impact on the environment and the preservation of cultural traditions, both of which need to be addressed.

Governments play a vital influence in the process of shaping the tourism industry through the application of various regulations. They ensure the prudent and sustainable growth of the tourism industry through the implementation of legislation, tax policies, and industry oversight. It is the mission of tourism promotion agencies, at both the national and the local level, to increase the number of tourists in order to stimulate economic expansion.

Cultural and Natural Resources: In order to be successful as tourist attractions, a lot of places rely on the natural beauty of their surroundings, in addition to their rich cultural histories. It is essential to the continued health of the tourism industry that these assets be guarded and preserved.

The Significance of the Economy:

Income Generation: The tourist business is responsible for the generation of a significant amount of income and makes a sizeable contribution to the gross domestic product (GDP) of many nations. The dollars that tourists spend on things like lodging, meals, mode of transportation, and a variety of attractions are then directly deposited into the local economy.

Opportunities for Gainful Employment One of the most major generators of jobs is the Tourism Industry. It is the primary source of income for millions of people all over the world, including those working in hotels and restaurants, as well as those providing transportation services and guiding tourists. The tourist industry is a significant source of employment in many nations; as a result, it contributes to the overall reduction of unemployment while also fostering the development of a more varied labor force.

Diversification of the Economy: Tourism frequently plays a catalytic role in the process of economic diversification. Small enterprises, local entrepreneurs, and communities in both urban and rural regions are able to generate income from it as well as take advantage of the opportunities it presents. This type of diversification increases economic resilience and stability, particularly in geographic areas that have historically relied on a single industry.

Impact on Culture as well as the Environment:

Exchange of Cultures: Tourism is a facilitator of cultural understanding and interaction between people of different backgrounds. When people travel, it gives them the chance to completely submerge themselves in different cultures, traditions, and ways of life, which helps them develop empathy, tolerance, and appreciation for diversity. The interactions that tourists have with local people, the cultural activities in which they take part, and the cuisines of the region all contribute to the formation of personal bonds that are not limited by borders and help to develop goodwill across nations.

Preserving cultural traditions is important since a large number of vacation spots rely on their cultural history to draw tourists. The cash generated by tourism can be used to pay the maintenance and refurbishment of historical landmarks, museums, cultural events, and traditional customs. This contributes to the preservation and promotion of a region's cultural identity.

Environmental Conservation Despite the fact that tourism can result in negative environmental impacts if it is not appropriately managed, it also has the potential to be a driving force in environmental conservation. It is common practice for natural wonders, national parks, and animal reserves to rely on funds produced by tourism in order to finance conservation activities. Programs that maintain ecosystems, protect endangered species, and encourage sustainable resource management are funded by entrance fees, contributions, and sustainable tourist practices.

Concerning Difficulties and Controversies:

Overtourism has emerged as a critical problem in a number of vacation spots all over the world. When an excessive number of visitors visit a certain area, it can result in environmental deterioration, overcrowding, and strain on the infrastructure of the host country. The problem of overtourism requires solutions that strike a balance between the positive aspects of tourism and environmentally conscious business practices.

Community Conflicts Tourism can occasionally result in tensions arising between vacationers and the communities in which they stay. Dissimilarities in conduct, cultural misunderstandings, or an unfair distribution of economic gains can all contribute to strained relations.

Impact on the Environment Negative tourist practices can have a negative impact on the environment, including the destruction of natural ecosystems, the generation of pollution, and the overexploitation of natural resources. The goal of sustainable tourism is to lessen the impact of these unintended consequences.

Appropriation of Culture: The tourism sector has a responsibility to address concerns linked to cultural appropriation, which occurs when elements of local culture are used for commercial gain without providing proper respect to the communities from whom they originated. This can lead to the commercialization of cultures as well as their inaccurate depiction.

1.2 Key Components of the Tourist Economy

The tourism industry is a dynamic and varied sector that is essential to the functioning of the overall economy on a worldwide scale. It comprises a vast variety of businesses and services, all of which are geared toward satisfying the prerequisites and preferences of tourists. This essay investigates the fundamental aspects of the tourism industry, illuminating the myriad of fields that play a role in the expansion and significance of this sector of the economy.

Hospitality and Accommodations: Hotels, motels, resorts, and other types of lodgings make up the hospitality industry, which is an essential component of the economy that revolves around tourism. During their travels, guests can choose from a variety of accommodations, ranging from inexpensive hostels to opulent resorts with five stars, at these places. The hospitality industry is responsible for the employment of millions of people all over the world and relies on variables such as location, amenities, and the quality of service to attract guests.

Transportation is an additional component that is of critical importance. The tourism industry relies heavily on modes of transportation such as air travel, trains, road networks, and maritime connections. It is the responsibility of airlines, cruise lines, and public transportation agencies to make it as easy as possible for tourists to reach their destinations. In addition, in order for tourists to effectively explore their destinations of choice, ride-sharing apps and rental car companies have become increasingly important.

Services Related to Food and Drink: The gastronomic experience is an essential component of the tourism industry. Tourists can get a flavor for the culture of a place by eating at one of the many restaurants, cafes, street vendors, or food trucks that provide both regional and international cuisine. In recent years, there has been a rise in the number of people participating in culinary tourism. These tourists are looking for genuine and one-of-a-kind dining experiences.

Tour Operators and Travel Agencies: Both tour operators and travel agencies offer assistance to vacationers in the process of trip planning. They simplify the process of trip preparation by offering packages that include transportation, accommodations, and guided excursions all in one convenient package. Those individuals who would rather not negotiate the complications of travel on their own would find these services to be of particular use.

Entertainment and Attractions: Both entertainment and attractions play a significant role in the tourism industry's overall success. The overall tourism experience can be enhanced by visiting attractions such as museums, theme parks, historical sites, theaters, and sporting events. In order to preserve their standing as tourist destinations, these sites frequently call for ongoing care and financial contributions.

Retail & Shopping: Shopping is a common activity for tourists, and they may go in search of luxury goods, apparel mementos, or other types of goods. Important aspects of the economy that depend heavily on tourism are duty-free stores, street markets, and malls. They not only bring in cash but also support and encourage the development of local industry and craftsmanship.

A large number of vacationers are looking for one-of-a-kind and exciting experiences throughout their travels. Some examples of these kinds of activities are scuba diving, hiking, and safaris. A major increase in travelers' awareness of the importance of protecting natural resources and maintaining a healthy environment has led to the growth of the adventure and ecotourism industries.

Traveling is all about discovering new places, and one of the best ways to do so is by learning about the history and culture of the places you visit. Visitors who are interested in gaining
knowledge about the history and customs of a region are drawn to a location's historic sites, museums, and cultural events. This component contributes to the preservation of cultural assets and encourages cultural interaction.

Tourism for Wellness and Health Wellness and health tourism have been increasingly popular in recent years, as an increasing number of people seek opportunities to relax, rejuvenate, and receive medical treatment. This rapidly expanding industry requires the presence of spas, wellness retreats, and medical facilities in popular tourist areas.

MICE tourism refers to events, conferences, and exhibitions that are hosted in a variety of locations across the world. MICE stands for "meetings, incentives, conferences, and exhibitions." It draws in huge groups of people who want housing, meeting facilities, and entertainment, therefore it is a substantial contributor to the tourism economy.

Infrastructure for Tourism: The expansion of the tourist industry requires adequate infrastructure, which should include airports, highways, public transportation, and communication networks. Infrastructure must be continuously improved and expanded in order to support the growing number of tourists, and this task falls to both public and private investors.

Marketing and Promotion: Marketing and promotion efforts that are successful play an essential part in the process of luring tourists. Many different marketing approaches are utilized by national tourism boards, travel firms, and online platforms in order to highlight the distinctive characteristics of a location and encourage tourists to vacation there.

Services for travelers: During their trips, travelers can take advantage of a wide variety of services, including tour guides, translators, and travel insurance. The provision of helpful information and assistance by tourist information centers and mobile applications contributes to an experience that is more streamlined and pleasurable.

Participation of Communities and Locals: Participation of local communities is essential to the development of sustainable tourism. Community-based tourism programs aim to give local inhabitants with economic possibilities, protect cultural heritage, and empower local residents.

Regulation and Long-Term Sustainability: Governments play an important part in regulating the tourism industry to promote equitable business practices, public safety, and the preservation of the natural environment. As more people look for environmentally friendly and socially responsible vacation spots, sustainable practices are becoming more and more crucial.

Technology and Online Platforms: The development of technology and the proliferation of online platforms have radically altered the travel and tourism industry. Booking platforms, review websites, and travel applications have made it much simpler for vacationers to organize their travels and communicate with one another about their experiences.

Emerging Trends: The tourism industry is being reshaped by a number of new trends, some of which include the emergence of experiential travel and voluntourism as well as the influence of social media on vacation choices. These developments have an effect on the ways in which businesses and locations engage with tourists and attract new ones.

1.3 Benefits of Tourism

The tourism sector has several facets and confers a great number of advantages not only on tourists but also on the locations that tourists visit. It has developed into one of the greatest and most rapidly expanding economic sectors in the world, making a considerable contribution to the overall GDP as well as to the generation of new jobs and the dissemination of cultural traditions. In this paper, we will discuss the many positive aspects of tourism, including its economic and social benefits, as well as its contributions to the conservation of culture and the preservation of the natural environment.

Economic Expansion: Travel and tourism are major contributors to the expansion of the economy. Revenue is produced as a result of the money spent by tourists on things such as lodging, transportation, food, entertainment, and shopping. This infusion of money generates employment opportunities in a range of industries, including the hospitality industry, the retail sector, and the service industry. In addition, tourism has the potential to encourage the expansion of locally owned companies, which in turn can contribute to the general economic development of a location.

Opportunities to find work can be found in the tourist business, which is consistently ranked as one of the largest employers on a global scale. It affords employment opportunities to a diverse group of individuals, including those who work in hotels and restaurants, as well as those who are self-employed and sell handicrafts and souvenirs. These jobs frequently help local communities and can bring the unemployment rate down, particularly in areas that rely largely on tourism for their economic stability.

Exchange of Cultures: Tourism acts as a catalyst for cultural exchange by bringing together individuals from a variety of various origins. When people travel to new places, they are able to better understand and appreciate the local culture, traditions, and history of such places. In return, the communities that serve as hosts benefit from more exposure to other ideas and traditions, which fosters greater mutual understanding and tolerance.

Tourism's Potential Role in Fostering Cultural Heritage Conservation Tourism has the potential to foster cultural heritage conservation by acting as a catalytic agent. The upkeep and renovation of historical monuments, museums, and cultural events are frequently made possible thanks to the cash that is generated from tourism. The economic worth of conserving a community's cultural assets may become apparent to the community, which may lead to the preservation of those assets for future generations.

Infrastructure Development: In order to accommodate tourists, places frequently invest in the development of their infrastructure. Not only do tourists profit when local airports, roads, public transportation, and communication networks are upgraded, but local inhabitants do as well. These improvements have the potential to both encourage economic growth and raise the quality of life for the community that is being hosted.

Governments get the benefits of tourism by increasing their revenue from taxes and fees collected from visitors. The taxes that tourists pay on their lodging, transportation, as well as goods and services, all contribute to the money that the government receives. This cash has the potential to be put toward funding public services, education, and upgrades to infrastructure.

Agriculture, artisanal production, and food manufacturing are only a few examples of the kind of local businesses that benefit from tourism's promotion of these vocations. It frequently invites travelers to partake in regional food and purchase goods created in the area. This enables local farmers and artisans to generate cash, which in turn helps to boost the economy of the surrounding area.

Environmental Conservation Despite the fact that tourism can have adverse effects on the surrounding environment, it also has the potential to encourage people to participate in conservation initiatives. Natural and protected areas are frequent destinations for tourists, and the entrance fees paid by visitors help fund conservation efforts. In addition, tourism has the potential to increase people's understanding of how critical it is to protect the environment and its ecosystems.

Education Across Cultures: Travel and tourism are powerful tools for bridging cultural divides and fostering mutual understanding. When someone travels, they get the chance to interact with individuals from a variety of various backgrounds, learn new languages, and experience new and interesting cultures and traditions. These kinds of experiences contribute to the growth of a society that is more interconnected and aware of the outside world.

Tourism can provide a varied income stream for locations that have limited economic resources, making it an attractive industry choice for these kinds of locations. This type of diversification can assist lessen a community's reliance on a single industry or resource, so making the community more resistant to the effects of economic upheaval.

An Improved Standard of life One of the most common side effects of tourism's positive economic effects is an improvement in the population of tourist areas' standard of life. Those who live in these locations may experience an improvement in their quality of life as a result of increased job possibilities, enhanced infrastructure, and the expansion of existing local enterprises.

promoting Mutual Understanding and Cultural Exchange Tourism has the ability to promote peace and diplomacy by promoting a greater level of mutual understanding between people of different cultures. It is possible to help eliminate prejudice and improve international relations by encouraging people from different countries to connect with one another and learn from one another.

Positive Effects on Physical and emotional Health Wellness tourism, which can include activities such as spa getaways, yoga, and wellness centers, can have a beneficial impact on both the physical and emotional health of travelers. It affords one the chance to rest, re-energize, and get some much-needed reprieve from stress.

Opportunities for Education: Educational possibilities can frequently be found in the tourism industry. During their travels, tourists gain information about a variety of areas, including history, geography, ecology, and a host of others. Experiences that are educational can be found in museums, cultural institutions, and on guided tours.

Development on a Social and Community Scale Tourism has the potential to contribute to social development by instilling a feeling of civic pride and increasing community involvement. Residents of a town are often brought together during events, festivals, and other cultural activities planned for visitors, which helps to reinforce the community's social fabric.

Although there are many benefits to be gained from tourism, it is vital that its growth be managed in a responsible manner in order to avoid the possible adverse effects on the environment, local populations, and cultures. To reap the benefits of tourism without jeopardizing the destination's long-term health and prosperity, it is essential to implement sustainable tourism practices. These activities should center on the preservation of the destination's distinctive characteristics, the conservation of resources, and the minimization of negative consequences.

1.4 Challenges of Tourism

Tourism is a dynamic and ever-growing industry, but it also has a plethora of issues that can have far-reaching implications on destinations, communities, and the environment. Although tourism is a vibrant and ever-growing industry, it also faces a myriad of challenges. While tourism can be beneficial to the economy and the exchange of cultures, it also has the potential to put a burden on existing infrastructure, result in excessive development, and have unintended adverse effects on society and the environment. In the following paragraphs, we will discuss the considerable issues that the tourist industry faces, as well as the significance of tackling these challenges in order to ensure a responsible and sustainable industry.

Overcrowding and Overtourism: These two issues represent one of the most significant concerns confronting a great number of popular tourist locations nowadays. During the busiest times of the year, well-known tourist destinations and cities frequently see an influx of people that causes traffic jams, extends the amount of time spent waiting, and generally makes the trip less enjoyable for tourists. In addition, excessive tourism can place a strain on the area's natural resources and physical infrastructure.

Degradation of the Environment The tourism industry has a significant negative impact on the environment. Some examples of how tourism may be harmful to the environment include increased carbon emissions from air travel, excessive use of water resources, deforestation for the building of infrastructure, and pollution from cruise ships. These are just some of the examples. Both climate change and the degradation of habitats provide significant challenges to the world's ecosystems and biodiversity.

Erosion of Culture: Rapid tourism growth can lead to cultural erosion since traditional behaviors and beliefs are frequently changed or commodified to appeal to tourists. This can be a contributing factor in the loss of cultural identity. The distinct cultural identity of a location can be weakened when there is a loss of authenticity as well as an increase in the presence of influences from other countries.

Impact on Infrastructure The arrival of a large number of visitors can have a negative impact on a location's infrastructure, which can include its transportation networks, sewage systems, and waste management. Infrastructure that is operating at capacity may result in decreased efficiency, increased expenses, and a deterioration of the surrounding natural environment.

Inequality on Social and Economic Levels Although tourism has the potential to generate economic possibilities, it also has the potential to exacerbate existing levels of social and economic inequality. It is possible that local populations will not always benefit equally from the influx of tourist funds into a region. It is possible that jobs associated to tourism give low wages, which can lead to a widening of wealth gaps, particularly in developing nations.

Price Inflation: The demand for tourist places can lead to price inflation, making it difficult for local residents to afford essential products and services. This in turn makes it more difficult for tourists to visit those destinations. This can make economic disparity even more severe and lower the quality of life for people already living in the destination.

Loss of Authenticity: Authentic experiences are something that many tourists want for when they travel, yet the drive to meet the expectations of visitors can result in the loss of the destination's authenticity. When places put an emphasis on catering to large numbers of tourists rather than attempting to maintain their distinct identities, they run the risk of becoming indistinguishable from one another.

Seasonality and Unemployment Seasonal tourism can lead to jobs that come and go throughout the year. During the off-season in locations that are extremely dependent on tourism during certain times of the year, a significant number of workers are either unemployed or underemployed. This can result in difficult economic times for the communities involved.

Overdevelopment and Urbanization: In the effort to accommodate an increasing number of tourists, locations may turn to overdevelopment and urbanization in their efforts to meet their needs. This can result in the devastation of natural landscapes as well as the disappearance of cultural and historical points of interest.

Appropriation of Culture Tourism has the potential to propagate cultural appropriation, which occurs when aspects of one culture are appropriated without understanding or respect for another culture, typically for the sake of financial benefit. Insensitivity to other cultures and inaccurate portrayals of them might result from this.

worries Regarding Safety and Security The inflow of tourists can also raise safety and security worries for those who are traveling as well as for locals of the area. Criminals may find it simpler to carry out their activities in areas with larger crowds, and tourist sites may have a harder time assuring the safety of their guests as a result.

Insufficient laws and Enforcement Lax or insufficient laws and enforcement can make many of the problems that are already linked with tourism significantly worse. This includes concerns for the protection of the environment, the rights of workers, and the standards of safety.

Both natural catastrophes and the effects of climate change can have a negative impact on tourist destinations. Tourist hotspots are frequently at danger from natural disasters, and the effects of climate change can make these risks much worse. Tourism can be negatively impacted by natural disasters such as hurricanes, floods, and wildfires, as well as other severe weather conditions.

Concerns Regarding Health Emergencies on a global scale, like as the COVID-19 pandemic, have brought to light the susceptibility of the tourism business to issues that are associated with one's health. Tourism has been significantly impacted as a result of limits placed on travel, worries regarding personal safety, and the possibility of disease transmission.

Depletion of Resources Tourism has the potential to contribute to the depletion of resources, notably water resources. It may be difficult for popular places that are experiencing water shortages to provide residents and visitors with sufficient supplies of drinkable water.

Insensitivity to Other Cultures The insensitivity to other cultures and disrespectful behavior on the part of tourists can lead to conflict between visitors and the people they are visiting. Incidents of cultural insensitivity have the potential to tarnish the reputation of a location, which un turn can have a detrimental effect not only on the experience of tourists but also on locals.

Tourism methods that are responsible to the environment and sustainable are absolutely necessary in order to overcome these difficulties. When it comes to the environment, local people, and cultural heritage, the goal of sustainable tourism is to have as few negative effects as possible while making as many beneficial contributions as possible. In addition to this, it places an emphasis on the significance of educating tourists, including locals, and planning for the long run.

In addition, governments, local authorities, and the tourist industry need to collaborate in order to create and enforce policies that safeguard the environment and ensure the well-being of the communities that are hosts. Plans for the management of tourism, visitor quotas, and the creation of sustainable infrastructure can all contribute to the attenuation of the negative effects of tourism.

1.5 Economic Models in Tourism

The tourism business is incredibly intricate and varied, and it makes a considerable contribution to the economy of the entire world. The behavior of tourists, destinations, and the tourism industry as a whole can be better understood, analyzed, and predicted with the help of a number of different economic models. In this paper, we will investigate a variety of economic models in the tourist industry, each of which provides a distinctive viewpoint on the economic dynamics of this important sector of the economy.

Model of the Multiplier Effect:

The tourism industry relies heavily on the multiplier effect as its primary economic model. This demonstrates how an initial influx of spending inside a location can have a ripple effect, resulting in future rounds of economic activity being generated. When a traveler visits a location and spends money there, whether it is on lodging, mode of transportation, the cost of their meals, or activities, that money makes its way through the local economy. It helps maintain employment and commercial enterprises, encourages further expenditure, and makes a contribution to the region's general economic expansion. The multiplier effect is a useful method for gaining an understanding of the economic impact that tourism has on a location and measuring the magnitude of this impact in terms of the number of jobs that are created and the amount of money that is generated.

Model of Inputs and Outputs:

The input-output model is a more precise version of the multiplier effect that provides a quantitative study of how changes in tourism spending impact other sectors of the economy. This model was developed by economists at the University of Florida. This model splits the economy down into its component industries and illustrates the interdependencies that exist among those industries. It is possible for researchers and policymakers to evaluate the potential effects of changes in tourist spending on specific industries, such as transportation and hospitality, by first gaining a knowledge of the interdependencies that exist between these industries. This analysis is absolutely necessary for the tourism industry's strategic planning and decision-making processes.

TSA stands for Tourism Satellite Account

The Tourism Satellite Account is an all-encompassing economic model that may be utilized to determine the direct in addition to the indirect economic benefits that tourism makes to a certain region or country. It offers a structure that is both methodical and standardized, making it possible to collect and organize data on economic activity related to tourism. The TSA takes into account not only the conventional aspects of tourism, such as accommodations and transportation, but also the industry's more widespread influence, which may be felt in areas such as agriculture, construction, and retail. This model facilitates informed decision-making on the part of policymakers and other stakeholders about the distribution of resources and investments in tourist industry growth.

The Model of Supply and Demand:

The supply and demand model is a fundamental economic framework that investigates how prices and quantities are determined in a market. The model looks at how prices and quantities are determined in a market. When applied to the industry of tourism, this model assists in comprehending how the costs of travel services (such as airplane tickets and hotel rooms), among other examples, are established based on supply and demand considerations. It makes it possible to conduct an examination of the elements that influence both the decisions that suppliers in the tourism industry make and the behaviors of consumers. Stakeholders can make pricing and marketing tactics more effective by assessing supply and demand in order to better understand market dynamics.

Model of the Demand for Tourism:

Models of tourism demand investigate the factors that play a role in the decisions and actions of tourists. These models account for a wide range of demand-related factors, including income, prices, demography, and individual preferences. When destinations and businesses have this information, they can better customize their marketing efforts, the products and services they offer, and the prices they charge to attract and keep tourists. Demand models are particularly helpful in predicting how changes in external factors, such as the state of the economy or exchange rates, may have an effect on the behavior and spending of tourists.

Models for Tourism Prognostication:

Forecasting models for tourism make use of statistical methods and data from the past to make predictions about future tourism patterns.

These models are crucial for tourism-related destinations as well as enterprises operating in that industry. Forecasting models are able to estimate future demand and supply for tourism services by examining historical data. This data includes patterns of attendance and seasonal variations in visitation. This information is helpful for a variety of planning purposes, including resource allocation, marketing campaigns, and capacity planning.

Models for the Evaluation of the Economic Impact:

The economic effects of certain tourism initiatives, events, or regulations can be quantified with the help of models that are used in economic impact assessments. In order to evaluate the economic viability and potential benefits of tourism-related projects, these models frequently make use of cost-benefit analysis. Assessments of economic effect help stakeholders have a better understanding of the possible return on investment for projects such as the construction of a new convention center or the staging of a large event.

Model of the Tourism Product's Life Cycle:

Understanding the development of tourism destinations and products can be accomplished through the application of the tourism product life cycle model. It suggests that tourist sites and products pass through a series of distinct stages, beginning with discovery and development and progressing all the way up to maturity and then deterioration. As a location or product develops, this model allows stakeholders to better foresee how changes in demand and competition will affect them. They are able to modify their plans and assure continuing success and sustainability if they grasp these dynamics and apply that knowledge.

Model of the Tourism Area's Life Cycle:

The tourism area life cycle model is quite similar to the product life cycle model, but its primary focus is on the growth and development of entire tourist destinations rather than individual products. It highlights stages such as exploration, involvement, development, consolidation, stagnation, and decline in a given situation. This approach is especially useful for destinations because it reveals ways in which they may control growth, diversify their product offerings, and adapt to shifting visitor patterns over time.

Models of Tourism That Are Sustainable:

The Triple Bottom Line (TBL) and the Destination Stewardship Model are two examples of sustainable tourism models that attempt to strike a balance between economic, environmental, and social sustainability in the tourism industry. These models take into account the effects that tourism development will have in the long run on the communities, natural resources, and cultural traditions of the surrounding area. They place an emphasis on responsible practices that aim to reduce the destination's negative effects as much as possible while maximizing the positive contributions it receives.

Model of Tourism Losses Due to Leakage

The tourism leakage model analyzes the amount of money that "leaks" out of an economy due to the presence of tourists at a particular location. It is especially pertinent for developing countries that are extremely reliant on the tourism industry.

Leakage happens when a considerable amount of the money spent by tourists is funneled toward enterprises that are owned by non-locals or toward goods and services that are imported, rather than being invested in the domestic economy. This model shows the necessity of reducing leakage and retaining a greater portion of the revenue generated by tourism within the location.

Model of the Tourism Value Chain:

The model of the tourism value chain analyzes the many different phases and actors that are engaged in the production and distribution of goods and services related to tourism. It is beneficial to stakeholders because it helps them determine where in the supply chain costs are incurred and where value is added. Both locations and companies have the potential to improve their levels of profitability and competitiveness if they work to optimize the value chain.

Chapter 2

The Local Economic Impact

The tourism industry is a big contributor to the overall economy and plays an essential part in the growth and prosperity of a great deal of the world's geographical areas. It has the ability to promote economic growth, lead to the creation of employment opportunities, and contribute to an overall improvement in the wellbeing of the communities in which it is implemented. The direct and indirect impacts of tourist spending, job creation, infrastructure development, and the encouragement of local industries are all included in the local economic impact that tourism has. Other elements that contribute to this impact include a variety of other aspects. This all-encompassing study investigates the myriad ways in which tourism affects local economies, delving into its positive aspects as well as its drawbacks and proposing solutions for achieving long-term economic growth.

Impact on the Economy, Directly:

The immediate consequences of visitor spending within a location are what are meant to be referred to as the "direct economic impact of tourism." This covers money spent on lodging, meals and other beverages, transportation, entertainment, and shopping. When vacationers spend their money in these areas, they immediately contribute to the revenue and success of the businesses located in the community. For instance, the money made by hotels, restaurants, and souvenir stores not only keeps those businesses afloat but also serves as a source of tax revenue for the governments of the areas in which they are located. The increase in local community economic growth can be directly attributed to the direct economic impact, which can be measured as an increase in sales, earnings, and tax revenues.

Production of Employment Opportunities:

The tourism industry is a key source of job opportunities, providing work in a variety of fields including hospitality, transportation, retail, and entertainment. To properly attend to the needs of vacationers, businesses such as hotels, restaurants, travel agencies, and souvenir stores need to have a staff. In addition, the building and upkeep of tourism infrastructure, such as hotels and attractions, generates employment possibilities within the construction sector. The employment opportunities that are created by the tourism industry contribute to the reduction of unemployment rates, particularly in locations where there may be a scarcity of other work alternatives. This rise in employment not only makes it possible for individuals and families to maintain their financial security, but it also makes a contribution to the community's overall social and economic development.

The Development of Small Businesses:

The expansion of tourism frequently leads to the birth of new small enterprises that are geared toward satisfying the requirements of vacationers. The demand for genuine and locally made goods is beneficial to the local economy, particularly for farmers, craft dealers, and artists. In addition to giving possibilities for small business owners to generate revenue, souvenir stores that sell handcrafted goods, regional specialties, and cultural relics are important to the maintenance of local customs and heritage. It is crucial for the creation of a diverse and thriving tourism economy that represents the one-of-a-kind cultural uniqueness of the destination to provide assistance and promotion to the small enterprises that make up that economy.

The Development of Infrastructure:

The growth of tourism in a community can be a major impetus for the construction of new public facilities. The requirement to provide accommodations for an increasing number of tourists frequently results in expenditures being made in public amenity spaces, transit networks, highways, and airports. Not only does an improvement in infrastructure make the trip more enjoyable for tourists as a whole, but it also has a positive impact on the lives of local inhabitants by making it easier for them to access vital services and amenities. In addition, the development of infrastructure results in the creation of additional employment possibilities in the construction and maintenance industries, which in turn contributes to the expansion of the local labor force's contribution to economic growth.

Contribution to the Financial Stability of Local Government:

Taxation on tourism in its many forms—including sales tax, occupancy tax on hotels, and fees charged by tourist attractions—brings in considerable sums of money for the jurisdictions in which it is practiced. These funds make a contribution to the budgets of the local governments, which can then be used to fund public services, infrastructure projects, educational and medical facilities, and so on. As a result of the flood of tourist spending, the burden placed on local taxpayers is reduced, and the general financial health of the community is improved as a result of the contributions made by tourism-related earnings. In addition, investments in public services and infrastructure help not just tourists but also local inhabitants, contributing to an improvement in the quality of life for the entire community as a whole.

The protection of cultural traditions and historical artifacts:

The positive effects of tourism on the economy are not limited to monetary gains and the generation of new jobs. Additionally, it is of critical importance in the protection of cultural assets as well as the maintenance of regional customs. A great number of vacation spots are famous among travelers for its one-of-a-kind cultural offerings, historic landmarks, and customary activities. The development of cultural tourism not only results in the generation of cash but also serves as an incentive for the preservation and upkeep of these cultural resources.

It is common for local communities to be motivated to preserve their cultural heritage when they realize that doing so will become an essential component of the tourism product and will contribute to the identity and appeal of the location.

Effect of the Multiplier:

When discussing tourism, the term "multiplier effect" refers to the cumulative influence that is caused by tourist expenditure as it is redistributed across the economy of the host community. When tourists spend money on local products and services, the money that is generated by local companies is then spent on further local goods and services, creating a virtuous cycle that benefits the entire community. This ongoing practice of re-spending generates a chain reaction, which ultimately results in an economic impact that is far wider in scope than the initial expenditures made by tourists alone. The multiplier effect demonstrates the interconnectivity of many sectors in the local economy and stresses the importance of tourism as a driver for economic growth and development. Additionally, the effect highlights the interconnectedness of various sectors in the global economy.

Probable Obstacles and Possible Countermeasures:

Development of Tourism That Is Sustainable:

It is essential to put sustainable tourism strategies into action if one want to reduce tourism's detrimental effects on both the natural environment and the communities that it visits. This entails fostering efforts for ethical tourism, protecting natural resources, and cutting down on carbon footprints. The development of sustainable tourism places an additional emphasis on the significance of community involvement and empowerment. This ensures that local residents take part in decision-making processes that have an impact on their means of subsistence as well as the surrounding environment.

Diversification of the Products Offered by the Tourism Industry:

It is imperative to engage in product diversity within the tourist industry if one want to lessen the susceptibility of local economies to shifts in the demand for tourism. Promoting non-traditional types of tourism including ecotourism, cultural tourism, and adventure tourism can fall under this category. Destinations can appeal to a wider market and reduce the risk of being dependent primarily on mass tourism or seasonal tourism by providing visitors with a diversified choice of experiences to choose from.

Planning and Administration of the Infrastructure:

It is essential to have effective infrastructure design and management in order to meet the rising needs of the tourism industry while simultaneously reducing the burden placed on local resources. This includes making investments in environmentally friendly modes of transportation, waste management facilities, and technologies that reduce energy use. In order to avoid problems associated with overcrowding and the degradation of the natural environment, infrastructure planning should also take into account the carrying capacity of the destination.

Engagement with the Community and Efforts to Empower Its Members:

Involving local communities in the process of planning for tourism can help cultivate a sense of ownership and responsibility among members of such communities. The participation of community members in conversations on tourism development projects, cultural preservation, and sustainable practices can lead to the establishment of a sense of stewardship as well as the creation of shared goals. Community-based tourism programs provide local residents more influence by giving them economic options and encouraging them to preserve their cultural legacy. These efforts are centered on the local community.

Authenticity and preservation of cultural traditions:

It is absolutely necessary to maintain the originality of the local culture and traditions in order to produce a tourism experience that is singular and captivating. It is easier to demonstrate the genuine traditions and practices of a location when the local craftspeople, performers, and cultural practitioners are given more opportunities to take part in tourism-related events. It is possible to make a contribution to the maintenance of cultural identity and the reduction of cultural erosion by raising tourists' awareness of local customs and traditions and urging them to respect those traditions.

Building People's Capacity and Developing Their Skills:
Investments in education and the development of skills are absolutely necessary if one want to improve the level of competitiveness possessed by the local workforce in the tourism sector. Individuals can be equipped with the required abilities to succeed in a variety of tourism-related positions by participating in training programs, taking vocational courses, and taking language classes. To guarantee that communities are able to make the most of the job opportunities offered by the tourism industry, it is important to strengthen the capabilities of the local workforce through various capacity development projects.

The positive economic effects of tourism on a community can be broken down into a number of subcategories, including direct and indirect contributions to the economy, the generation of new jobs, the improvement of existing infrastructure, and the protection of cultural assets.

Revenue generation, the stimulation of employment, and the creation of chances for small enterprises are all direct results of tourism's significant contribution to the overall economic growth of local communities. However, tourism also presents issues, such as the degradation of the environment and cultural erosion, as well as congestion, which need to be addressed by the implementation of sustainable practices, the engagement of the local community, and the development of a long-term strategy.

Destinations are able to maximize the positive economic impact of tourism while mitigating the negative effects it has by adopting strategies that emphasize sustainable tourism development, diversification of the tourism product, infrastructure planning, community engagement, cultural preservation, capacity building, and responsible tourism initiatives. Case studies of prosperous tourist sites indicate the efficacy of the aforementioned tactics in attaining economic growth, conserving the environment, and preserving cultural identities.

It is vital that local communities, governments, and stakeholders work together to find a balance between economic development and the responsible and sustainable management of tourism as tourism continues to expand. This balance must be achieved as tourism continues to evolve. To ensure the continued prosperity of the tourism industry over the long term, it is necessary to carefully cultivate a number of interdependent aspects, including the economic health of nearby communities, the protection of natural resources, and the maintenance of cultural traditions and artifacts.

2.1 Local Economies and Tourism

Tourism is a big economic factor that has a significant impact on the economics of local communities all over the world. When tourists visit a location, they spend money there, which stimulates the local economy, benefits a diverse range of local companies, and generates new employment opportunities. At the same time, local communities are responsible for providing the fundamental infrastructure, services, and attractions that are necessary to attract tourists. This symbiotic link between tourism and local economies is one that is dynamic and multifaceted, featuring benefits as well as obstacles.

Positive Effects on the Economies of the Area:

Creating New Jobs:

The generation of new jobs is one of tourism's most important and substantial contributions to the economies of local communities. The industry provides employment opportunities in a wide variety of fields, including the hospitality business, the transportation industry, the retail sector, and cultural attractions. Tourism is essential to the economic well-being of a wide variety of local companies, including hotels, restaurants, tour operators, and artisanal producers.

Because of the variety of career prospects, inhabitants of the area have access to a wide variety of positions, ranging from those in customer service to those in management and administration.

Earnings from Customers:

Both municipal governments and private businesses benefit monetarily from tourism's economic impact. Taxes that tourists pay on their accommodations, services, and purchases provide revenue that can be used for public services, the expansion of infrastructure, and community improvement initiatives. Increased sales are beneficial to local companies, and the additional revenue that results is important to the firms' continued viability and expansion. As a result of its support for community-based services and amenities, this infusion of funds can contribute to the preservation and enhancement of the residents' quality of life.

Expanding of Small Businesses:

The expansion of smaller enterprises is frequently a byproduct of the expansion of the tourism industry. The demand for genuine and locally made goods can be beneficial to the local economy, particularly for farmers, craft sellers, and artists. Small company entrepreneurs have the opportunity to succeed in a variety of contexts, including souvenir stores that sell handcrafted goods, regional specialties, and cultural relics. This not only helps to diversify the local economy but also to develop a one-of-a-kind and lively tourism experience that is reflective of the cultural uniqueness of the place.

The Development of Infrastructure:

Destinations routinely invest in the improvement of their infrastructure in order to better serve the requirements of tourists. Enhancements to airports, transit networks, roads, and public amenities not only improve the experience for tourists as a whole but also confer benefits on the people who live in the area. Investing in infrastructure results in improved access to important services as well as the creation of more job opportunities in the building and maintenance industries, all of which contribute to the expansion of the regional economy.

Effect of the Multiplier:

The concept of a "multiplier effect" in tourism refers to how a single round of spending at a destination can lead to several subsequent rounds of spending and subsequent economic activity. When tourists spend money on goods and services offered by local companies, the money that is brought in by those purchases is then invested back into the community. The initial expenditures made by tourists are only the beginning of the economic impact that is caused by this cyclical process, which results in a ripple effect. The multiplier effect highlights the interconnection of many sectors within the local economy and accentuates the role that tourism plays as a stimulant for the growth and development of the economy.

Probable Obstacles and Possible Countermeasures:

While tourism does provide a number of economic benefits, it also creates a number of issues that need to be addressed in order to assure the industry's continued viability and reduce the amount of damage done to local economies.

Too Many People and Too Many Tourists:

Overcrowding is a common problem in popular tourist locations, which can put a strain on local resources, lead to traffic congestion, and have a severe impact on the quality of life of local residents. Destinations have the ability to impose visitor limits, control access to sensitive locations, and promote off-peak and alternative attractions in order to mitigate the effects of this difficulty. It is imperative to have efficient management of the location if one wishes to maintain a steady flow of tourists.

Deterioration of the Environment:

It is possible for tourism to have a negative impact on the surrounding environment, such as an
increase in carbon emissions, the destruction of habitat, and an over use of natural resources. Sustainable tourism activities are required in order to reduce the negative impact that tourism has on the surrounding ecosystem. These measures include eco-friendly transportation, waste

reduction, and wildlife conservation efforts. Protecting local ecosystems also requires fostering environmentally responsible tourism practices and educating tourists and travelers about the importance of environmental preservation.

The Degradation of Culture:

The rapid growth of tourism can lead to the loss of cultural traditions since traditions and values of the host community are frequently transformed or commercialized to appeal to tourists. Cultural preservation should be a top priority for management of destinations, and they should pursue projects that highlight real customs and heritage. Protecting and maintaining a community's cultural identity can be facilitated by activities such as fostering community-based tourism and including locals in decision-making processes.

The rise in general prices:

The demand brought forth by tourism can cause prices to rise, making it difficult for local residents to afford even the most fundamental goods and services. This can make existing economic disparities worse and bring to a decline in the people' quality of life. Price restriction, diversification of the tourism product, and services that cater to a range of budgets should all be at the forefront of the mind of those in charge of managing the destination, since they are the best ways to prevent excessive price inflation.

Concerns Regarding Health:

The tourism business has been brought into the spotlight as a vulnerable sector as a result of

global health issues such as the COVID-19 epidemic. In order to address health issues, destinations are required to place an emphasis on both safety and hygiene. It is essential to provide prompt responses to health emergencies and maintain clear communication in order to regain the confidence of travelers. Increasing resiliency in the face of health-related disturbances is another benefit that can be gained from diversifying tourism offerings beyond mass tourism and seasonal peaks.

Insensitivity to other cultures:

Insensitivity to local culture on the part of tourists can aggravate relations between those tourists and the communities they visit. Cultural awareness and sensitivity can be fostered through the implementation of educational and training programs that are open to locals and visitors alike. It is possible to lessen the adverse effects of tourism on society by putting an emphasis on cultural sensitivity in advertising and by promoting cultural events that are conducted responsibly.

Tourism has a dynamic and symbiotic relationship with the economics of local communities. This link presents potential for economic expansion, the creation of new jobs, and the maintenance of cultural traditions. Although tourism offers many advantages, it also creates a number of difficulties that need to be managed in a responsible manner. Destinations have the ability to optimize the good economic impact of tourism while limiting the negative implications it may have by implementing sustainable practices, diversifying the tourism offering, and incorporating local populations in decision-making processes.

The lessons that may be learned from prosperous locations and the methods that have proven to be the most effective highlight the significance of cultural preservation, environmental conservation, and responsible tourism. Local communities are able to utilize the economic power of tourism for the long-term benefit of their citizens as well as the protection of their cultural and natural assets if they pay special attention to and carefully nurture the balance between economic development and sustainable tourism.

2.2 Measuring Economic Impact

It is crucial for businesses, governments, and decision-makers to have a solid understanding of the economic impact of the myriad of activities, industries, and events that occur. It makes it possible to make educated decisions about planning, the allocation of resources, and assessments of an economy's general health and ability to remain sustainable. This study investigates the methodologies and approaches that are used to evaluate economic impact, with a particular emphasis on the ways in which these assessments assist us in improving our decision-making across a variety of settings.

1. **Methods for Assessing and Measuring the Economic Impact: Analysis of Inputs and Outputs:**
    The analysis of inputs and outputs is a quantitative tool that is used to examine the interdependencies that exist between the various parts of an economy. It provides a quantitative analysis of how shifts in one industry affect others, so enabling the calculation of direct, indirect, and induced effects on the economy. Because this method provides an all-encompassing view of the ripple impact of economic activity inside an economy, it is particularly useful for studying the effects of particular industries or events.
    Analysis of the Multiplier Effect:
    The multiplier effect is a method for calculating the amount of additional economic activity that is brought about by a change in spending levels. This is frequently done in order to evaluate the effects of the expenditures, investments, or events carried out by the government. One dollar spent might result in more than one dollar's worth of economic impact thanks to the multiplier effect, which takes into account both direct and indirect consequences.
    Analysis of Costs and Benefits (CBA):
    Comparing a project's expenses with its potential gains is the basis of a cost-benefit analysis, which determines the initiative's overall influence on the economy. It is frequently utilized in the process of evaluating infrastructure projects, policies of governments, and investments. CBA enables decision-makers to establish the total economic feasibility and desirability of a project by quantifying not just the financial costs and benefits, but also the non-financial costs and advantages of the initiative.
    Taking Part in Polls and Questionnaires:
    Data can be collected directly from individuals, corporations, or

organizations through the use of surveys and questionnaires. Insights about consumer behavior, preferences, and spending habits can be gained with the use of these, which can be adapted to meet the specific needs of particular research objectives. The economic impact of events, tourism, and consumer behavior can be better understood through the use of surveys, which are particularly valuable in this regard.

An Examination of Regression:

The statistical technique known as regression analysis is used to investigate the connections that exist between various variables.

When used to the context of measuring the economic impact of something, it can be used to determine how shifts in the value of one variable (like a new policy, for example) affect the value of another variable (like employment or sales, for example). Identifying correlations and basing predictions on previous data are both possible through the use of regression analysis.

The Social Accounting Matrices, or SAMs, are as follows:

SAMs are complete data frameworks that provide a detailed depiction of an economy, including the interactions between various economic agents (households, enterprises, government, etc.) and sectors. SAMs are also referred to as system dynamics models (SDMs). SAMs are also helpful for modeling economic implications on a macroeconomic scale, which makes it easier to comprehend how income, production, and consumption are distributed.

Analysis of the Economic Impact:

An examination of the fiscal impact looks at the impacts that actions taken by the government have on revenue and expenses. It analyzes how different policies, including alterations to tax rates or incentive programs, affect the growth of the economy as well as the finances of the government. An consideration of the fiscal impact is necessary for both the design of budgets and the evaluation of public policies.

2. Measurement of the Economic Impact in Different Sectors and Contexts:

Tourism:

An economic impact analysis is typically utilized in the process of determining the extent to which tourism contributes to local and national economies. This involves calculating the amount of money brought in by tourists' spending, the number of jobs that are created, and the indirect effects that tourism has on allied industries like the hospitality and transportation industries. Studies on the impact of tourism enable destinations to evaluate the relevance of their tourism business and make educated decisions on marketing, the development of infrastructure, and the distribution of resources.

Celebrations and Gatherings:

It is vital to conduct economic impact assessments in order to have a knowledge of the economic advantages that can be gained from hosting events, festivals, and conventions. These studies attempt to quantify not just the direct spending of guests but also the indirect spending that has a rippling impact on local companies. Event organizers and local governments can use event impact evaluations as a reference when it comes to the planning and marketing of events, as well as when deciding whether or not to host similar gatherings in the future.

The Development of Infrastructure:

It is absolutely necessary to do an economic effect analysis prior to making any governmental or private investments in infrastructure projects. The feasibility and attractiveness of projects such as transportation improvements, public transit systems, and energy facilities can be determined with the assistance of cost-benefit analysis. Because infrastructure projects can have far-reaching effects on the economy, precise assessment is of the utmost importance.

The World of Entertainment and Sports:

In order to illustrate the benefits of stadiums, arenas, and sporting events, the sports and entertainment industries rely on economic impact assessments. These studies investigate the financial effects on the local economy, including the number of jobs created and the amount of tax money collected. An economic impact analysis is one of the tools that may be used to win public support and get funding for entertainment and sports businesses.

Policies Adopted by the Government:
Cost-benefit analysis and fiscal impact analysis are two methods that governments employ in order to evaluate the various policies' effects on the economy. Changes to tax policy and efforts to improve healthcare are two examples of these initiatives. The evaluation of the possible consequences on government income, economic growth, and public welfare can be aided by economic impact measurements.

Conventions and Other Unique Occasions:
Visitors who spend money on things like lodging, food, and other services are a significant contributor to the growth of local economies that are stimulated by special events, trade exhibitions, and conventions. Studies of economic effect quantify the monetary gains and new job opportunities that result from the occurrence of these gatherings. These studies are relied on by event organizers, convention centers, and local companies to assess the worth of hosting such events in their respective locations.

3. **The Significance of Determining the Extent of the Economic Impact:**

   The Art of Making Informed Decisions:
   When economic effect is measured, decision-makers receive data-driven insights into the repercussions of their actions, which helps them make better decisions. For the purpose of making well-informed decisions, it is vital to have a solid grasp of the economic implications of any course of action being considered, whether it be the planning of a new infrastructure project, the

introduction of a new policy, or the staging of an event.

Distribution of Resources:

The economic impact study helps to ensure that resources are distributed effectively. When governments, organizations, or enterprises invest in projects or events, they want to ensure that the resources they are allocating are being directed toward the efforts that will generate the highest economic advantages. Measuring impact allows for more effective prioritization of spending.

Support and funding from the public sector:

Studies of the economic impact typically play an important part in the process of securing public support and funding. Investors, taxpayers, and other stakeholders can be persuaded to support a particular project or sector by demonstrating the financial benefits of the project or business. The presentation of convincing economic facts is an important step toward securing financial support for initiatives.

The Planning for Economic Growth:

It is necessary, while planning for long-term economic growth, to have a solid understanding of
the economic impact of the various industries and activities. It is helpful in identifying sectors of the economy that are strong as well as those that need attention or improvement. These kinds of information are especially helpful for governmental bodies tasked with economic development and for developing regional regions.

Evaluation of Public Policy:

Measurement of a policy's economic impact is an essential component of its overall effectiveness analysis. Policymakers evaluate whether particular actions have had the anticipated effects on the economy, which enables tweaks, revisions, or entire policy changes to be made as necessary.

4. **Concerning Obstacles and Restrictions:**

Availability of Data and the Quality of It:

The availability and quality of data are two critical factors that influence how accurately economic impact is measured. Because the data may be restricted or out of date in some instances, it can be difficult to carry out assessments that are thorough.

Various Predictions and Assumptions:

Many different assumptions and factors are involved in the modeling of economic impact. The accuracy of the results is dependent on the validity of these assumptions, which might be difficult to verify, which in turn depends on the accuracy of the assumptions.

Differences Between Causation and Correlation:

It might be difficult to establish a causal relationship between a particular action or occurrence and the economic impact that it has. Studies of economic impact frequently base their conclusions on correlation rather than causation, therefore it is essential to evaluate the findings with extreme caution.

Factors from the Outside:

Economic effects can be impacted by a variety of external causes, including but not limited to global economic conditions, natural disasters, and technology advancements. It can be difficult to identify the specific impacts that are caused by a single element.

The possibility of bias:

It is possible for economic impact studies to be biased, particularly when they are commissioned by groups who have a financial stake in the outcome. In order to guarantee the reliability of the findings, it is necessary to employ open research practices and methodology.

The measurement of economic impact is an essential instrument for gaining a knowledge of the repercussions that various actions, fields of endeavor, and public policies have. It contributes to the processes of decision-making, the distribution of resources, and the evaluation of the efficacy of projects. Despite the fact that measuring the economic impact comes with its fair share of difficulties and restrictions, it is nevertheless a vital step in the process of making well-informed decisions that foster economic expansion, stability, and sustainability. For an economic impact study to be successful, it is necessary to make use of proper methods and data, to be transparent, and to have a solid comprehension of the economic environment as a whole.

2.3 Job Creation and Local Development

The production of new jobs is a primary catalyst for community development, having an effect not only on economic expansion but also on the general wellbeing of the community. When jobs are produced within a community, it leads to a number of positive effects, some of which include an increase in income, a reduction in unemployment, improved social conditions, and an overall enhancement of prosperity. The importance of the mutually beneficial link that exists between the formation of new jobs and the advancement of local communities cannot be overstated.

Growth of the Economy:

The development of new employment opportunities is a primary driver of economic expansion at the regional level. When existing businesses grow or when new enterprises set up shop in a community, they not only bring investments but also produce revenue and encourage economic activity. This ultimately results in a rise in local GDP as well as production and consumption.

The development of new jobs helps to inject money into the local economy, which in turn encourages the expansion of other types of businesses and services. This creates a virtuous cycle that drives economic growth.

Lower Rates of Unemployment:

The most effective strategy to address unemployment, which is one of the key difficulties faced by local communities today, is to create more job opportunities. People are able to provide for themselves and their families, find work when there are job opportunities, and work when there are job opportunities. A drop in the unemployment rate leads to a lessening of the costs associated with social welfare and an improvement in the quality of life generally.

Production of Cash Flow:

The creation of jobs locally immediately adds to the generating of revenue for citizens of the area. Individuals who have steady job are in a position to earn a paycheck, which enables them to provide for themselves and raises their overall standard of living. When people in a community have higher wages, there is a greater likelihood that they will spend more money overall and that they will patronize local businesses, both of which will further stimulate the local economy.

Developing One's Capabilities:

Increasing one's level of education and experience is frequently necessary in order to create new jobs. This not only ensures that local workers are better equipped to fulfill the demands of the job market, but it also gives chances for personal development and professional progress for those individuals. The ability of a workforce to be competitive and adaptable in a local economy is enhanced by the worker's level of education and skill.

Stability within the Community:

The stability of the community is essential to the growth of the community, and employment creation helps encourage that stability. When people have steady work, they are more likely to put down roots in a place, make an investment in homeownership, and participate in civic and social activities in their neighborhood. This stability helps create social relationships and a sense of belonging, both of which are beneficial to the development of the local community.

Tax Collections:

Creating new jobs helps local governments bring in more money through various forms of taxation. When people and companies make money, they are required to pay taxes. These funds can then be used to finance public services, the expansion of infrastructure, and various community improvement endeavors. The community as a whole will reap the benefits of the important services that are funded thanks to these revenues.

Economies that are both Diverse and Sustainable:

The creation of local jobs through economic development helps to encourage economic variety. Local economies that are diversified over a variety of industries and sectors are better able to weather swings in the national and local economies. A more diversified economy is one that is more resilient and sustainable, which in turn lowers the community's susceptibility to economic downturns.

Entrepreneurship and creative problem solving:

The production of jobs in a community serves to stimulate both innovation and entrepreneurial activity. Entrepreneurs frequently arise from the ranks of the existing labor, bringing with them novel concepts, goods, and services to the market. The expansion of entrepreneurial endeavors and the creation of new employment opportunities both contribute to the growth of thriving local economies.

2.4 Infrastructure Development

The construction of new infrastructure is an extremely important factor in the stimulation of economic growth, the enhancement of living standards, and the promotion of social well-being. It comprises a wide variety of physical assets and infrastructure that are essential to the operation of societies, such as communication systems, transportation networks, energy supply, water and sanitation services, public amenities, and so on. This in-depth study examines the relevance of developing society's infrastructure, as well as its primary components, the problems that come with doing so, and the role that it plays in sculpting affluent and resilient civilizations.

The Significance of the Development of Infrastructure:

Competitiveness and the Promotion of Economic Growth:

The nation's economic growth and competitiveness are both supported by the nation's infrastructure. The movement of both goods and people is made easier by well-developed transportation networks, which may include roadways, trains, and airports. This in turn helps to support trade and commerce. The effective operation of businesses, the promotion of innovation, and the facilitation of connectivity within and between areas all depend critically on the availability of dependable energy and communication networks. The expansion of a nation's infrastructure increases its competitiveness in the global investment market, boosts the number of available jobs, and propels economic output.

Improvements Made to Connectivity and Accessibility:

The construction of infrastructure improves connectivity and accessibility, making it easier for individuals and communities to gain access to important services, employment opportunities, and other social amenities. It is easier to gain access to education, healthcare, and markets when there are well-functioning transportation networks that cut down on travel times and expenses. Connectivity is increased when people have access to reliable sources of energy and communication services. This enables individuals to engage in the global economy and get knowledge that can improve the quality of their lives.

Enhancement of the Overall Quality of Life:

The development of infrastructure has a profound impact on both the quality of life of individuals and the quality of life of communities. The availability of clean water and services for sanitation contributes to improvements in public health by lowering the incidence of diseases transmitted by water and enhancing general well-being. Residents' physical and emotional well-being is improved when adequate housing, public parks, and recreational facilities are provided. This helps to cultivate a feeling of community and promotes the cohesiveness of the community as a whole.

Development in Urban and Rural Areas:

The construction of critical infrastructure is essential for both urban and rural communities. A well-planned infrastructure in urban centers helps to support population expansion, reduces the amount of congestion that residents experience, and improves the general livability of cities. Infrastructure projects in rural regions, like roads, electrification, and irrigation systems, have the potential to increase agricultural output, provide access to markets, and narrow the gap between rural and urban living conditions.

Resistance to adversity and long-term viability:

It is vital to make investments in infrastructure that is both robust and sustainable in order to face the problems that are posed by climate change and natural disasters. Communities are better able to withstand and recover from environmental shocks when they have infrastructure that is climate-resilient. This type of infrastructure includes flood protection systems, sustainable water management, and energy-efficient transportation. In addition to fostering environmental sustainability and mitigating the effects of climate change, the development of environmentally responsible infrastructure also helps reduce carbon emissions.

Important Elements in the Construction of Infrastructure:
Infrastructure pertaining to transport:

Roads, highways, bridges, trains, airports, and seaports are all components of the nation's transportation infrastructure. It makes it easier to move people, commodities, and services, which opens the door to opportunities for commerce, tourism, and overall economic growth. It is essential to have transportation networks that are well connected in order to support and ensure the seamless movement of commodities as well as regional and worldwide trade.

Infrastructure for Energy Supply:

The three main components of energy infrastructure are power generation, power transmission, and power distribution. Coal, natural gas, hydroelectric, solar, and wind power are all examples of conventional and renewable energy sources that are included in this category. For the purpose of providing support for industrial activity, residential requirements, and technological breakthroughs, it is vital to have energy infrastructure that is both reliable and efficient.

Infrastructural Support for Communication:

The telecommunications networks, internet connectivity, and digital technologies that make up communication infrastructure are all interconnected. It makes it easier for people to communicate with one another, it boosts online business, and it promotes worldwide communication. The availability of dependable communication infrastructure is absolutely necessary for the promotion of economic growth, technological advancement, and social advancement.

Infrastructure for the Provision of Water and Sanitation:

The term "water and sanitation infrastructure" refers to the networks that deliver water, the facilities that process wastewater, and the sanitation services itself. For the sake of community health, illness prevention, and overall prosperity, having access to clean water and adequate sanitary facilities is absolutely necessary. Infrastructure that provides sufficient water and sanitation contributes to improved living conditions and a population that is in better health.

Accommodations and Community Facilities:

The term "housing infrastructure" refers to residential buildings, as well as community facilities and affordable housing initiatives. Amenities available to the public, such as schools, medical centers, parks, and recreational facilities, all contribute to the overall livability of a community by encouraging people to engage with one another and taking care of their health.

Development of Critical Infrastructure Faced with the Following Challenges and Opportunities:

Constraints Placed on the Budget:

The difficulty of insufficient money is a significant obstacle in the process of developing infrastructure. It is imperative that international organizations, private investors, and national governments work together to successfully raise sufficient funds for infrastructure projects. Bonds on existing infrastructure, public-private partnerships, and international collaboration are all potential ways to assist close the funding gap and support the expansion of existing infrastructure over the long term.

Frameworks for Both Policy and Regulation:

When it comes to fostering the development of infrastructure that is both sustainable and resilient, having effective policy and regulatory frameworks is absolutely necessary. It is necessary for governments to formulate unambiguous laws, simplify cumbersome regulatory procedures, and cultivate an atmosphere that encourages engagement from the private sector. When it comes to luring investments and guaranteeing the smooth execution of infrastructure projects, having governance that is open and honest as well as having regulatory clarity are both essential.

Adoption of Technology and Innovative Practices:

It is essential to make use of cutting-edge technologies and pioneering approaches in order to ensure the effective and environmentally responsible development of infrastructure. The use of intelligent infrastructure solutions, digitization, and technologies that utilize renewable energy sources can improve the infrastructure systems' capacity for resiliency, efficiency, and environmental sustainability.

The Impact on the Environment and Society:

The development of infrastructure may have enormous repercussions on both the environment and society. When planning sustainable infrastructure, environmental conservation, social inclusion, and community engagement are all important factors to take into consideration. The conduct of environmental impact assessments, engagement with local populations, and the implementation of strategies for green infrastructure can all contribute to the attenuation of the negative effects of development on ecosystems and communities.

Management of Assets, Including Maintenance

When it comes to ensuring the longevity of infrastructure systems and maximizing their effectiveness, effective maintenance and asset management are absolutely necessary.

It is imperative to put into practice efficient maintenance plans, make investments in asset management systems, and train a qualified personnel if one want to maintain the performance of infrastructure assets while also ensuring their safety.

Adaptability in the Face of Climate Change and Natural Disasters:

The growing number of natural disasters that are attributed to climate change presents a substantial obstacle for the construction of new infrastructure. The implementation of disaster risk reduction measures and the construction of infrastructure that is resistant to the effects of climate change are two of the most important things that can be done to reduce the vulnerability of people and the systems that support them. It is absolutely necessary to incorporate climate adaption measures into the planning and design of infrastructure if one wishes to ensure its long-term sustainability and resilience.

The Importance of Infrastructure Development to Long-Term Economic Growth:

The creation of new physical infrastructure is essential to the achievement of long-term economic growth and social advancement. Infrastructure systems that are well-planned and properly managed contribute to the general well-being and resilience of communities. This is accomplished through the promotion of connectivity, the improvement of productivity, and the enhancement of the quality of life. In order to construct a future that is more inclusive, resilient, and sustainable, it is vital to make strategic investments in the development of infrastructure, which should be backed by solid policies, new technology, and sustainable practices.

Chapter 3

Tourism and Small Businesses

The tourism industry is a major driver of the global economy, making important contributions to GDP, employment, and cultural interaction. In this all-encompassing research, we dig into the complex relationship that exists between tourism and small companies. Specifically, we investigate the ways in which tourism has an effect on small businesses, the opportunities it provides, and the obstacles that small company owners confront when operating in the tourism industry. Our goal is to provide a comprehensive understanding of the role that small businesses play in the tourism industry by focusing on a variety of issues, such as the provision of lodging and food services, artisanal goods, and guided tours.

1. **The Role That Tourism Plays in the Success of Small Businesses**
   Contribution to the Economy:
   When it comes to the tourist industry, small companies are a major driving force that contribute to the overall economic vibrancy of destinations. Many small businesses, such as family-owned

restaurants, family-owned motels, and local artisan stores, are able to thrive in areas that are popular with tourists because of the patronage that they receive from tourists. These companies not only contribute to the local economy via the generation of money but also through the production of employment possibilities.

Various Products and Services:

The travel experience is improved as a whole thanks to the wide variety of goods and services that are provided by the small businesses that operate within the tourist industry. These businesses provide guests genuine, off-the-beaten-path experiences that distinguish a place in a variety of ways, such as providing travelers with distinctive lodging options and regional cuisine, handcrafted souvenirs, and personalized guided tours.

Protecting Our Cultural Heritage:

The maintenance and continuation of local customs and traditions are frequently dependent on the contributions made by smaller companies. The preservation of a destination's cultural character is assisted by the presence of artisanal craft shops, cultural performances, and heritage-centered tours. This preservation of culture contributes value to the whole tourism offering and attracts tourists who are looking for an authentic experience.

Community Involvement:

Small enterprises in the tourism industry are typically owned and operated by inhabitants of the surrounding community. Because of the strong ties that exist between the tourism industry and the local community, a sizeable amount of the cash that is created by tourism stays within the confines of the local economy. Local business owners typically have a vested interest in the well-being of their communities and are more inclined to engage in activities that promote social responsibility.

2. **Possibilities within the Tourism Industry for Small Businesses Services Relating to Lodging:**

Travelers who are looking for a more personalized and distinctive housing experience will find that small hotels, bed & breakfasts, and vacation rentals are ideal options. They frequently give a degree of service and attention to detail that larger hotel companies may find difficult to achieve for their guests. These companies are able to contact customers all over the world because to their partnerships with online platforms such as Airbnb and Booking.com.

Tourism in the Culinary Arts:
By providing real regional cuisine and ingredients produced locally, local restaurants, cafes, and food vendors have the opportunity to capitalize on the growing trend of culinary tourism. The appeal of the location is increased, and opportunities for culinary entrepreneurs are created, through activities such as food tours, cooking workshops, and themed dining experiences.

Handmade Goods & Traditional Keepsakes:
Tourist hotspots provide fertile ground for the growth of artisanal businesses that specialize in the production of handcrafted goods and mementos. These establishments give tourists the opportunity to purchase one-of-a-kind wares crafted regionally, thereby assisting regional craftspeople and encouraging cross-cultural interaction.

Operators of Tours and Other Activities:
The tourism experience relies heavily on locally owned and operated small businesses that offer a variety of tours and activities, including guided city walks, outdoor experiences, and cultural outings. Because of their in-depth knowledge of the surrounding area and their commitment to providing individualized service, they are an invaluable asset to the sector.

Services Relating to Transportation:
The mobility requirements of tourists are met by a variety of local service providers, such as taxi and shuttle companies, businesses that hire bicycles, and shops that sell rental bikes. They improve

the convenience and accessibility of a location, which results in a more pleasurable travel experience.

3. **Obstacles Confronted by Small Businesses in the Tourism Industry**

   Demand based on the Season

   The difficulty of meeting seasonal demand is one that is faced by a great deal of tourism-related small enterprises. It is possible that certain months or times of the year, depending on the location, see a higher concentration of tourists than others. Due to the fact that seasonality can result in variable income, it can be challenging for firms to continue their operations throughout the entire year.

   The Competitors:

   The tourism sector is one that often features cutthroat competition, particularly in well-known vacation spots. When competing with larger organizations that have higher marketing resources and brand recognition, small businesses may find it difficult to compete successfully. To differentiate oneself from the competition, efficient marketing and distinction are needed.

   Obstacles Presented by Regulators:

   Small tourism firms may face regulatory hurdles, such as licensing requirements, zoning restrictions, and safety laws. These challenges can arise from a variety of sources. Regulatory landscapes like this one can be difficult to navigate, which can be both time-consuming and expensive, especially for young business owners.

   In terms of marketing and having a presence online:

   Establishing and sustaining your internet presence is absolutely necessary in order to successfully attract travelers in today's increasingly digital environment. There are a lot of small businesses, and most of them don't have the money or the ability to successfully sell themselves on the internet, which could potentially limit their reach.

   The costs of operations include:

Rent, utilities, staff pay, and upkeep are just some of the expenses that come along with operating a tourism-related small business. When business is slow or the economy is in a slump, it can be especially difficult to maintain a healthy balance between revenue and expenses.

4. **Tourism Business Tactics for Startups and Small Companies**

Platforms for Online Advertising and Reservations:

Establishing a solid online presence, complete with an easily navigable website and active

social media profiles, is essential for the success of small businesses. Working along with other online booking platforms, such as Airbnb, Viator, or Booking.com, can help to extend their customer base.

Differentiation Based on Market Niche:

Catering to specific subsets of the market is one way for smaller firms to set themselves apart. Travelers who are looking for one-of-a-kind experiences are likely to be interested in specialized offers such as eco-tours, art courses, or gourmet excursions.

Working Together and Making Connections:

Cooperation between local firms, particularly smaller ones, can result in the formation of partnerships that are mutually beneficial. For instance, a boutique hotel can form a partnership with a local eatery to provide guests with access to unique package deals.

Participation in Community Activities:

Participating actively in the community where one lives can help cultivate support and loyalty. Participating in community events, sponsoring local initiatives, and obtaining goods and services from local vendors are all options open to small businesses.

Practices That Promote Sustainability:

It is possible to attract tourists looking for environmentally friendly and socially responsible experiences by promoting sustainable tourism practices and responsible travel policies. Small firms can differentiate themselves from their competitors by adopting responsible business practices and green initiatives.

When it comes to the tourism industry, small companies are extremely important contributors to economic expansion, the maintenance of cultural traditions, and community involvement. Even though they face many obstacles, such as fluctuating demand throughout the year and intense rivalry, small businesses in the tourist industry have the opportunity to succeed by separating themselves from the competition, making use of online platforms, and developing partnerships. The success of platforms like as Airbnb, Viator, and Etsy highlights the potential for small enterprises to access a consumer base that extends across the globe.

3.1 Role of Small Businesses in Tourism

In the travel and tourist industry, the unsung heroes are the little enterprises. Small businesses, such as family-run restaurants, boutique hotels, and local craftsmen and tour operators, are the ones that offer a substantial and one-of-a-kind contribution to the tourism industry. While large hotel chains and international corporations frequently steal the show, it is the former that are responsible for the latter. In the course of this in-depth investigation, we will investigate the crucial part that small businesses play in the tourist industry. More specifically, we will investigate their influence on regional economies, the variety of experiences they provide, the obstacles they must overcome, as well as their capacity for innovation and resiliency.

1. **The Role That Small Businesses Play in the Tourism Industry's Contribution to the Economy**
   Creating New Jobs:
   The tourism industry relies heavily on the employment opportunities provided by small businesses. There are a wide variety of small businesses that offer employment opportunities; some examples of these are bed-and-breakfasts, local eateries, tour operators, and boutique hotels. These professions frequently have

a significant focus on the local community, with owners hiring local citizens and contributing to lower overall rates of unemployment.

Earnings from Customers:

Revenue generated by locally owned and operated small enterprises helps to support and grow the local economy. These companies and their suppliers are helped by the money that tourists spend on things like lodging, food, sightseeing trips, and mementos. These expenditures, in turn, fund public services, the development of infrastructure, and community projects, all of which contribute to an improvement in the people' quality of life overall.

Experiences that are both Unique and Genuine:

The trip experience can be made more genuine and one-of-a-kind by patronizing local small businesses, which offer a wide variety of goods and services. Small businesses are frequently the first choice for vacationers who are looking for more personalized and culturally enriching activities during their trip. These activities can include staying in hotels owned by locals, eating regional food, participating in locally crafted activities, and touring local attractions.

Participation in the Community:

Many times, small enterprises have strong ties to the communities in which they operate. The establishment's proprietors and employees cultivate robust ties with the locals and guests, which can lead to increased involvement in the community. It's possible for small businesses to contribute to the sense of community by either taking part in or sponsoring local activities.

2. **The Possibilities and Obstacles Facing Small Businesses in the Tourism Industry**

    Occasions to seize:

    Targeting Specific Markets: Small businesses can find success by targeting specific markets by providing one-of-a-kind experiences, such as eco-tours, cooking classes, or cultural immersion programs. Travelers who are looking for genuine and unique experiences are drawn to these specialized services.

Small businesses have the ability to offer travelers experiences and packages with added value if they collaborate with other local businesses. For instance, a boutique hotel may work in conjunction with a neighborhood eatery to provide visitors with a one-of-a-kind dining experience.

Online Presence: By harnessing the power of the internet, small businesses have the ability to build an online presence, which allows them to reach a wider audience and simplify online bookings. The use of internet booking portals, review platforms, and social media platforms all have the potential to be effective marketing and customer interaction tools.

The Obstacles:

Demand that varies with the seasons affects a large number of small enterprises in areas that are popular tourist destinations. This can lead to inconsistent earnings and a precarious financial situation during the shoulder seasons.

Small businesses in important tourist areas face competition from larger hotel chains and corporations, both of which have huge marketing expenditures and strong brand awareness. Differentiation through inventive means is required in order to effectively distinguish oneself in a market that is highly competitive.

Costs of Operation: Running a small tourism business may be rather pricey. It is possible for expenses like as rent, utilities, and salaries of staff members to put a burden on the budget, particularly during times of poor business or economic crisis.

Regulatory Obstacles: Small businesses frequently encounter standards that are difficult to understand and that take up a lot of time. Small businesses in the tourism industry may encounter major obstacles in the form of licensing requirements, zoning restrictions, safety rules, and taxation.

When it comes to marketing and having a presence online, many small businesses may not
have the means or the experience necessary to effectively market themselves online. It might be difficult to construct an engaging online presence while simultaneously connecting with people all around the world.

3. Tourism Business Tactics for Owners of Small Establishments

Platforms for Online Advertising and Reservations:

It is essential to establish a solid presence on the internet. Websites that are easy to use, social media profiles that are regularly updated, and material and images of high quality should all be created by small businesses. Working along with other online booking platforms, such as Airbnb, Viator, or Booking.com, can help to extend their customer base.

Differentiation Based on Market Niche:

Catering to specific subsets of the market is one way for smaller firms to set themselves apart. Travelers who are looking for one-of-a-kind experiences are likely to be interested in specialized offers such as eco-tours, art courses, or gourmet excursions.

Working Together and Making Connections:

Cooperation between local firms, particularly smaller ones, can result in the formation of partnerships that are mutually beneficial. For instance, a boutique hotel can form a partnership with a local eatery to provide guests with access to unique package deals.

Participation in Community Activities:

Participating actively in the community where one lives can help cultivate support and loyalty.

Participating in community events, sponsoring local initiatives, and obtaining goods and services from local vendors are all options open to small businesses.

Practices That Promote Sustainability:

It is possible to attract tourists looking for environmentally friendly and socially responsible experiences by promoting sustainable tourism practices and responsible travel policies. Small firms can differentiate themselves from their competitors by adopting responsible business practices and green initiatives.

The tourism industry relies heavily on the contributions that small companies provide to economic expansion, the maintenance of cultural traditions, and the participation of locals. Even though they face many obstacles, such as fluctuating demand throughout the year and intense rivalry, small businesses in the tourist industry have the opportunity to succeed by separating themselves from the competition, making use of online platforms, and developing partnerships. The success of platforms like as Airbnb, Viator, and Etsy highlights the potential for small enterprises to access a consumer base that extends across the globe. In the end, small businesses that are involved in tourism have the potential to improve the overall travel experience by offering possibilities that are one-of-a-kind, individualized, and culturally enlightening for travelers. Their function in the tourism industry is not limited to the processing of transactions; rather, it entails the production of engaging and genuine experiences that encourage repeat visits from tourists and the expansion of local economies.

3.2 Support Systems for Small Businesses

Small businesses are the backbone of economies all around the world, making substantial contributions to the creation of new jobs, innovation, and the economic strength of their respective countries. It is crucial that they have a strong support system in place to ensure their success. In the course of this in-depth investigation, we will investigate the many different forms of assistance that are made accessible to small businesses. These can take the form of anything from financial aid and mentoring programs to technical solutions and government initiatives. Small businesses are able to triumph over obstacles, grow, and prosper when they are aware of and make use of the various support systems available to them.

1. **Availability of Financial Assistance**
   The Difference Between Grants and Loans:
   When beginning, growing, or recovering from financial setbacks, small enterprises frequently need access to finance. Loans and grants catered specifically to the requirements of small enterprises are made available by governments and other financial institutions. These funds are versatile and can be put to a variety of uses, including serving as operating capital, purchasing equipment, or conducting research and development.
   Microfinancing entails:
   Microfinancing institutions provide entrepreneurs with the opportunity to obtain small loans for a shorter period of time than is typically offered by traditional banks. These loans are a lifeline for entrepreneurs who do not have collateral or a credit history and are essential for the survival of small firms located in developing nations.
   Investors of the Angel Kind and Venture Capital:
   Capital is provided to startups and early-stage small enterprises by angel investors and firms that specialize in venture capital. They not only contribute financial resources, but also bring essential skills and possibilities for networking. These investors are essential to the development of high-potential startups and businesses that focus on technology.
2. **Career Guidance and Development of Businesses**
   Incubators and Accelerators for New and Existing Businesses:
   Startups and small firms can benefit from coaching, networking opportunities, and access to resources through the use of business incubators and accelerators. They offer an atmosphere conducive to the development of crucial skills, such as access to capital and the refining of business concepts, to aspiring business owners.
   The acronym for these places is "Small Business Development Centers."

Small Business Development Centers (SBDCs), which are frequently supported by the government, give small firms access to expert consultants who offer help on a variety of elements of running a business, such as business planning, marketing, and financial management.

Organizations for Networking:

It is easier for small firms to network with one another and work together when they belong to business networking groups like chambers of commerce, industry associations, and local business clubs. These networks offer the possibility of exchanging one's own experiences, discovering new mentors, and gaining access to various resources.

Programming for Mentoring:

Mentorship programs pair seasoned business owners and professionals with newly established entrepreneurs and professionals who are looking for advice. During the difficult stages of starting a business, these programs can provide emotional support as well as insights, guidance in problem-solving, and assistance in finding solutions.

3. **The Provision of Technological Assistance**

   Marketplaces available online:

   Online marketplaces such as Etsy and eBay give small businesses the opportunity to sell their wares to a wider audience at a lower cost than would be incurred by opening a physical storefront. They supply the necessary tools for product listings, monetary transactions, and communication with customers.

   Instruments of Digital Marketing:

   Small businesses may expand their online presence and communicate with clients more effectively with the assistance of digital marketing tools such as advertising on social networking platforms, email marketing, and search engine optimization. Reaching a specific audience with the assistance of these tools is an efficient use of resources.

Platforms for Electronic Commerce:
Small businesses now have the ability to open and operate their own online storefronts thanks to e-commerce platforms such as Shopify and WooCommerce. They provide capabilities for the administration of inventory, the processing of payments, and the fulfillment of orders.

Services Hosted on the Cloud:
Small businesses have access to a variety of resources, including those for communication, document collaboration, and data storage, thanks to cloud-based services such as Google Workspace and Microsoft 365. These services both increase productivity and make it easier to operate remotely.

4. **Initiatives Taken by the Government and Support for Policies**
Tax breaks and deductions:
Numerous countries alleviate the financial pressure placed on small enterprises by lowering their overall tax burden by providing tax incentives and deductions. These incentives can take the form of discounts for certain expenses, such as those associated with research and development, the acquisition of equipment, and the employment of particular groups, such as veterans or those with disabilities.

Programs for Obtaining Government Contracts:
Small businesses are given access to more government procurement possibilities through the use of programs that allot a certain percentage of total contracts to be awarded to smaller enterprises. These programs provide assistance to many different kinds of small companies, including those that are run by women, members of minority groups, and veterans.

Support for Regulatory Compliance:
The regulatory systems that apply to small firms can be made more straightforward and efficient by governments. It is possible to make it less difficult for small businesses to handle compliance requirements by lowering the number of bureaucratic barriers

and giving clearer directions.

Access to the Markets of Other Countries:
It is possible for governments to offer assistance to small enterprises in order to facilitate their entry into foreign markets. Growth on a worldwide scale can be aided by participation in trade promotion programs, trade missions, and access to trade agreements.

5. **Fostering Resilience and Offering Support in Times of Crisis**
   Planning for the Continuity of Business Operations:
   Small businesses have the opportunity to receive assistance in the process of building business continuity plans that will better equip them to respond to many types of emergencies, including pandemics, economic downturns, and natural disasters. They are able to continue their business and quickly recover thanks to these plans.

   Emergency Financial Aid and Relief Funds:
   In times of crisis, governments, charitable groups, and communities in the surrounding area may frequently support small companies with grants and relief cash to assist them in weathering the storm. These funds have the potential to cover necessary expenses as well as bridge any financial shortfalls.

   Programs for Emotional and Mental Health and Wellness:
   The emotional health and general well-being of those who run small businesses is frequently ignored. For business owners who struggle with anxiety and stress, participation in activities and programs designed to offer emotional and psychological support can be absolutely essential.

6. **Obstacles Facing the Support of Small Businesses**

Ability to be reached:
Support programs are neither universally known about or accessible to all of the nation's small companies. It is critical to work toward

achieving equitable access to support, especially for populations that have historically been at a disadvantage.

The Official Language of Bureaucracy:

The difficulty of the application procedure, the lack of clarity regarding qualifying requirements, and the length of the approval process can discourage small firms from seeking funding. It is absolutely necessary to streamline administrative processes.

Long-term viability:

There is a potential cause for concern regarding the viability of support services. It may be difficult to provide continuous, long-term support for certain initiatives because those programs may rely on limited funding sources or be sensitive to changes in political climate.

Altering Conditions in the Business World:

The landscape of business is continuously shifting as a result of developments in technology, upheavals in the economy, and crises on a global scale. It is imperative that support systems evolve in order to keep up with the ever-evolving requirements of small enterprises.

The development of new ideas, the production of new jobs, and overall economic expansion are all driven by the activities of the nation's millions of small enterprises. Their success and resilience are directly tied to the robustness of their support networks. Small businesses have a better chance of succeeding if they have access to several types of support, including financial assistance, mentoring, technical solutions, and government programs. Support systems may continue to empower small businesses by addressing difficulties such as accessibility, bureaucratic hurdles, and program sustainability. This will help to stimulate the growth of small businesses as well as enhance their role as vital contributors to both the local and global economies. The support of small businesses is not just an investment in those businesses specifically, but also in the health and wealth of the communities and nations in which they are located.

3.3 Success Stories of Small Businesses in Tourist Areas

TOURIST DOLLARS FUELING GROWTH IN LOCAL ECONOMIES

The travel experience is profoundly influenced and local economies are positively impacted by the presence of small enterprises in regions that are popular with tourists. These businesses, which are frequently distinguished by their one-of-a-kind items and individualized customer service, are not only holding on to their existence but also growing in locations where tourism is a big industry. In this section, we discuss the uplifting and motivational achievements of small enterprises located in a variety of tourist destinations that have shown resiliency, inventiveness, and a commitment to increasing the quality of the tourism experience.

1. **Maasai Beadwork Cooperatives, which are located in Kenya and Tanzania:**
   In the Maasai communities of Kenya and Tanzania, local women have banded together to form cooperatives that manufacture and sell traditional beadwork, jewelry, and other crafts. These cooperatives have also been successful in generating income for their members. The Maasai women who participate in these cooperatives have the opportunity to earn a sustainable income while also conserving their cultural traditions. It is possible for visitors to the region to purchase beautifully beaded jewelry and other handicrafts directly from the women who produce them, giving a shopping experience that is both genuine and considerate. These cooperatives have found success in catering to conscious travelers who are looking for one-of-a-kind mementos with a relevant backstory by combining the preservation of cultural traditions with economic emancipation.
2. **The Redwood Hyperion Suites, in the state of California, United States of America:**
   The Redwood Hyperion Suites is a cozy, family-run boutique hotel that can be found in Three Rivers, California. The Sequoia and Kings Canyon National Parks are literally right outside the hotel's front door. The dedication of this hotel to both the

preservation of the natural environment and the satisfaction of its guests is what separates it from other establishments. The proprietors have made investments in environmentally friendly methods such as solar panels and a program that eliminates garbage completely. In addition to providing visitors with the option to explore the awe-inspiring gigantic sequoia trees and surrounding hiking trails, they provide guests with a tranquil and all-encompassing experience in the heart of nature. The Redwood Hyperion Suites is a great example of how small companies may flourish by delivering one-of-a-kind, environmentally conscientious experiences in locations that are popular with tourists interested in ecotourism.

3. **Rice 'n Spice, located in the city of Chiang Mai in Thailand:**
   Rice 'n Spice is a modest cooking school in Chiang Mai, Thailand, that is maintained by a local family. This company stands out for its hands-on cooking workshops despite being located in a location that is well-known for the vibrant street food and culinary culture that it embodies. Travelers have the option to master the art of Thai cuisine by going to a local market, picking fresh ingredients, and preparing dishes under the direction of expert instructors. This experience can take place while they are in Thailand.

   Rice 'n Spice is a great example of how small businesses can capitalize on the growing industry of culinary tourism by providing experiences that are not only fun and tasty but also informative and entertaining for those who are passionate about food.

4. **Black Hops Brewing, located in Australia's Gold Coast:**
   Craft beer is brewed at Black Hops Brewing, which can be found in Australia's Gold Coast, a region that is quite popular among tourists. What began as a pastime among close friends has evolved into a thriving business that is well-known for the creative specialty brews it produces. The creators of the brewery embrace a culture of collaboration by inviting members of the

community to participate in the brewing process and frequently experimenting with novel flavor combinations. They have turned their passion for artisanal beer into a location that beer lovers and tourists absolutely cannot miss out on checking out. Black Hops Brewing is a shining example of how small businesses can succeed in highly competitive industries by putting an emphasis on quality, involvement in the local community, and creative problem solving.

5. **A tour of the island by tuk-tuk in Sri Lanka:**
Tuk Tuk Safari is a locally owned and operated tour company in Sri Lanka that provides visitors with an alternative and exciting way to discover the island. The company offers clients an exhilarating and genuine experience through the use of tuk-tuks, also known as auto-rickshaws. While traversing the breathtaking landscapes of Sri Lanka, tourists have the option of going on a number of tours, some of which include culinary adventures, cultural explorations, and wildlife excursions, among other things. The success story of Tuk Tuk Safari demonstrates the possibility for smaller tour operators to create unique, environmentally responsible, and adventure-driven experiences that are catered to tourists looking for unusual adventures.

6. **The Icelandic Lava Show, which may be found in Vik, Iceland:**

The Icelandic Lava Show, which can be found in the village of Vik in the south of Iceland, provides guests with an experience that is one of a kind and one that they will never forget. Guests will get the opportunity to see as molten lava is poured over ice as part of the display, which recreates the effects of a volcanic explosion. This attraction, which is owned by a family, has become popular among tourists looking to gain a greater understanding of the volcanic geology of Iceland while also experiencing an adventure that is both safe and fascinating. The success of the Icelandic Lava Show is a testament to the unique and instructive options that small enterprises may give to enrich the experience that tourists have when visiting a destination.

These examples of small businesses doing well in tourist locations are a reflection of the diversity and inventiveness of business owners who are succeeding in the cutthroat and always shifting environment that is the tourism industry.

These companies have found a way to appeal to the passions and requirements of vacationers by catering to their interests in cultural preservation, sustainable practices, gastronomic experiences, craft brewing, alternative modes of transportation, and educational excursions, respectively. Their successes can serve as a source of motivation for other small businesses, and they highlight the potential for creativity and differentiation, as well as a dedication to improving the quality of the travel experience in locations all over the world. The landscape of tourism is still being shaped in large part by the contributions of small enterprises, which continue to play an essential part by providing tourists with authentic and unforgettable experiences that leave an imprint that lasts.

3.4 Challenges Small Businesses Face

The creation of new jobs, new industries, and overall economic expansion are all considerably aided by the contributions made by the world's millions of small enterprises. Nevertheless, the road ahead for owners of small businesses is littered with a great number of obstacles. In the following in-depth investigation, we will investigate the most typical difficulties that are encountered by small firms. These difficulties might range from restrictive financial limitations and intense rivalry to burdensome regulatory requirements and personnel issues. Small business owners can manage the obstacles and establish resilient firms if they have a solid awareness of the issues they face and put into action effective tactics.

1. **Restrictions Caused by Money**
   Access to Financial Resources:

When trying to get the necessary finance for startup fees, expansion, or operations requirements, small firms frequently face challenges. Growth and innovation can be stifled when there is insufficient access to capital.

Administration of Cash Flow:

Keeping a positive cash flow can be a big difficulty for small firms, as these companies frequently deal with inconsistent streams of revenue and delayed payments from clients. Ineffective management of one's cash flow might put one in a precarious financial position.

Expensive Costs of Operation:

Expenses for running the business, such as rent, electricity, and compensation for employees, can put a burden on the budget, particularly during times of economic stagnation or poor business.

2. **The Market Place**

   Companies of a Considerable Size:

   When competing with giant organizations that have extensive marketing resources, established brand awareness, and economies of scale, small businesses frequently find it difficult to compete successfully. This can make it challenging for smaller businesses to acquire a larger part of the market.

   Competition Held Via the Internet:

   E-commerce and online marketplaces have thrown open the door to global competition, and as a result, it is absolutely necessary for small businesses to build a robust online presence in order to compete effectively in the digital arena.

   Competitors in the Neighborhood:

   Even in more insular areas, rivals on the local level might be a problem. The problem is to separate your company from its competitors and to bring in a base of loyal customers.

3. **Obstacles Caused by Regulations**

   A Complicated System of Licensing and Permitting:

For small firms, navigating the complexities of the criteria for licensing and permission may be a time-consuming and expensive endeavor. It is a considerable challenge to comprehend all applicable local, state, and federal regulations and to act in accordance with them.

The tax system:

When it comes to taxes, small businesses can face complicated regulations, which can include
a wide variety of deductions, credits, and compliance obligations. The process of tax planning and preparation can be extremely stressful.

Laws Governing Employment:

When it comes to employing and managing staff, small firms can run into difficulties as a result of employment restrictions such as labor laws, minimum wage requirements, and mandates for health insurance coverage.

4. **Promotion and Presence on the Internet**

    Constrained marketing spending budget:

    It is difficult for many small firms to compete successfully with larger companies because they have limited resources for marketing and promotion. This makes it difficult for small enterprises to reach a wider audience.

    Visibility on the Internet:

    In this day and age, it is absolutely necessary to establish and continue to maintain an internet presence. It can be difficult for small businesses to develop and maintain websites that are user-friendly, optimize their content for search engines, and interact with their consumers using social media.

    Management of One's Reputation:

    Small businesses can be severely harmed by critical comments made on social media platforms and online reviews that are negative. It might be difficult to preserve a good reputation in the digital space.

5. **Concerns Regarding the Workforce**
   Both New Employees and Keeping the Old Ones:
   It can be difficult for small businesses, particularly those operating in labor markets that are highly competitive, to find and keep talented staff. The turnover of employees can cause disruptions in operations and drive up costs.
   Staff Training and Development:
   Because small organizations typically have fewer resources available for employee training and professional development, it can be challenging to help workers expand their skill sets and encourage career advancement.
   Maintenance of a Healthy Work-Life Balance:
   The owners of small businesses frequently have difficulty striking a balance between their personal and work life. Burnout is a common result of working long hours and feeling constant pressure to keep the business afloat.
6. **Changes in the State of the Economy**
   Demand based on the Season
   The market for many types of goods and services tends to fluctuate seasonally, creating seasonality that affects many small enterprises. It's possible that seasonal enterprises will struggle when business is slow.
   Downturns in the Economy:
   Recessions and crises in the economy can provide substantial issues since they can result in decreased consumer spending and economic uncertainty, both of which can lead to financial distress and the closure of businesses.
7. **Developments in New and Emerging Technologies**
   Adoption of New Technologies:
   It can be challenging for smaller firms to keep up with the rapid advancement of technology. Putting money into new computer hardware, computer software, and digital infrastructure can be a challenging financial endeavor.

Security in cyberspace:
Because of their increasingly heavy reliance on digital technologies, small firms are increasingly susceptible to cyberattacks. Protecting sensitive data and information about customers is becoming an increasingly important problem.

8. **Engaging the Customer as Part of the Process**
   The Acquiring of Customers:
   It might be challenging to bring in new clients, especially in areas that are already very saturated. It can be difficult for small firms to distinguish themselves from their competitors and stand out.
   Retaining Current Clients:
   The process of establishing and sustaining loyal consumer relationships is a continual issue. It is crucial to provide constant value while also providing great customer service.

9. **Concerns Regarding the Environment and Sustainability**
   Practices That Promote Sustainability:
   It can be difficult to successfully promote sustainable and environmentally friendly practices, particularly with regard to the initial investments required and the education of end users.
   Regulations Regarding the Environment:
   There is a possibility that small enterprises will be required to comply with environmental standards. This may result in higher expenses and issues associated with compliance.

10. **Competition on a Global Scale**
    The era of globalization:
    When expanding into international markets, small firms not only have to contend with competition on the domestic front, but also on a global scale. The complexities of supply chain logistics, trade rules, and cultural differences can be challenging to navigate.

11. **Shifting Aesthetic Preferences of Consumers**
    The Latest Consumer Trends:
    Small firms need to be able to quickly adapt and invest in developing technologies in order to remain competitive in the face of

shifting consumer preferences, such as the trend toward sustainable products, contactless payments, and online shopping.

12. **The Disruption Caused by Technology**
    Disruption of an Industry:
    The advent of new technologies has the potential to shake up established markets and business models, forcing small companies to either adapt their operations or undergo a total paradigm shift.
13. **Emotional Health and General Well-Being**

Both Stress and Exhaustion:
The emotional health and general well-being of those who run small businesses is frequently ignored. There is a risk of stress and burnout as a result of the continual strain, long hours, and unpredictable financial situation.

Resilience, adaptation, and careful strategic planning are required to successfully navigate these hurdles. Small firms that are successful are frequently able to overcome these challenges by capitalizing on their distinctive advantages, such as their adaptability, specialized services, and involvement in their local communities. In today's highly competitive business environment, it is essential for small firms to have access to a variety of resources, including mentorship programs, support networks, and government programs specifically designed to help them succeed. In the end, despite the fact that the path may be difficult, small firms continue to be an essential component of the economic fabric of society, serving as a driver of innovation and producing chances for growth.

Chapter 4

Sustainable Tourism

The concept of sustainable tourism has evolved as an important paradigm for encouraging ethical travel habits and ensuring the continued protection of the natural environment, cultural traditions, and the socioeconomic status of the communities that are visited. Because the tourism sector throughout the world is still growing at a rapid rate, the implementation of sustainable business practices has become an absolute necessity in order to reduce the adverse effects of mass tourism. This all-encompassing investigation digs into the broad concept of sustainable tourism, investigating its fundamentals as well as its difficulties, ideal procedures, and examples of its application. We may pave the way for a more ecologically conscious and socially responsible attitude to traveling and enjoying leisure activities if we have a better understanding of the complexity of sustainable tourism as well as its value.

1. **Comprehending the Concept of Sustainable Tourism**
   The Meaning of the Term "Sustainable Tourism"
   Sustainable tourism, also known as responsible tourism or ecotourism, is the practice of developing and managing tourism

activities in a way that protects the natural and cultural authenticity of a destination while simultaneously creating economic and social advantages for the communities that are located there. It seeks to maximize the beneficial consequences of tourism, such as conservation, community empowerment, and cultural preservation, while minimizing the negative affects of tourism, such as environmental degradation, cultural commercialization, and economic leakage. The goal of this effort is to do this by balancing the two.

The following are the core tenets of sustainable tourism:
The idea of striking a healthy equilibrium between the many factors of environmental impact, sociocultural impact, and economic impact is central to the ideas of sustainable tourism. The reduction of carbon footprints, the promotion of local economies, the preservation of local cultures, the conservation of natural resources, and the encouragement of community engagement and empowerment are essential guiding principles.

The Importance of Ecotourism in Today's World:
The conservation of biological diversity, the maintenance of natural landscapes, and the security of cultural assets all depend on the practice of sustainable tourism. It encourages responsible consumer behavior, adds to the tourism industry's long-term viability, and helps maintain amicable relationships between visitors and the communities that welcome them.

2. **The Role of Tourism in Maintaining a Healthy Environment Vacation Rentals That Are Kind to the Environment:**
The hospitality industry is critically important to the development of environmentally responsible tourism. In order to leave as little of a negative impact on the surrounding environment as possible, eco-friendly lodging establishments like green hotels and eco-lodges adopt energy-efficient techniques, trash reduction strategies, and water conservation measures.

Protection of biodiversity and efforts toward conservation:

The preservation of natural environments and animal populations is a primary focus of sustainable tourism. The viewing of wildlife in a responsible manner, the protection of endangered species, and the restoration of habitat are all goals promoted by conservation efforts such as wildlife reserves, marine conservation areas, and national parks.

Fostering Environmentally Responsible Transportation:

As a means of lowering carbon emissions and fostering environmentally responsible transportation practices within tourist destinations, boosting the use of public transit, fostering cycling and walking tours, and making investments in electric or hybrid vehicles for tours and transfers all contribute to the reduction of carbon emissions.

The Administration of Waste and Recycling:

The reduction of pollution and the minimizing of the damaging effects of tourism on local ecosystems are both helped along by the implementation of efficient waste management and recycling programs in tourist locations. It is also very important to encourage travelers to dispose of their trash in an environmentally acceptable manner.

3. **The Role of Sustainable Socio-Cultural Practices in the Tourism Industry**

Regarding the Cultures of the Area:

The practice of responsible tourism entails showing respect for and making efforts to preserve local customs and cultures.

The socio-cultural sustainability of a location can be improved by participating in cultural exchange programs, encouraging real cultural experiences, and providing support to local artisans and craftsmen.

Empowerment of the Community:

Residents are able to actively participate in the tourism sector and benefit from the economic opportunities it brings when local communities are empowered via tourism initiatives such as community-based tourism and social entrepreneurship projects. These projects are made possible by empowering local communities through tourism initiatives.

The Protection and Preservation of Cultural Heritage:

It is absolutely necessary, in order to keep the cultural identity of a location intact, to take measures to preserve historical landmarks, monuments, and traditional architecture. The negative effects of over tourism and the commercialization of culture can be mitigated by employing sustainable tourism practices at cultural heritage sites. These strategies include the protection and promotion of these places.

Programs for Education and Social Awareness:

Educational programs and cultural awareness projects that are geared toward both tourists and the communities that host them help to build mutual understanding, respect, and appreciation. These programs have the potential to foster learning about other cultures, education about the environment, and appropriate behavior when traveling.

4. **The Tourism Industry's Impact on the Economy**

Development of the Community's Economy:

The creation of employment opportunities, the support of small enterprises, and the promotion of the purchase of locally produced goods and services are all ways in which sustainable tourism helps to contribute to the economic growth of local communities.

The Distribution of Revenue:

It is possible to promote a tourism economy that is both more inclusive and more sustainable by taking measures to ensure that tourism revenue is divided fairly among local stakeholders, such as owners of small businesses, entrepreneurs, and members of the community.

Putting Money Into the Infrastructure of the Community:

Investments in community infrastructure, such as transportation networks, healthcare facilities, and educational institutions, not only improve the overall quality of life for members of the community, but also create an atmosphere that is more conducive to the growth of sustainable tourism.

The Diversification of Tourism:

Promoting ecotourism, adventure tourism, and cultural tourism are all examples of diversified forms of tourism that can help spread the economic advantages of tourism more equitably and minimize the strain that is placed on major tourist destinations.

5. **The Obstacles Facing Sustainable Tourism and Its Limitations**

Striking a Balance Between Economic Growth and Conservation:

Finding a happy medium between environmental protection and tourism industry expansion is still one of the most difficult challenges facing sustainable tourism. To achieve this balance, it is generally necessary to engage in rigorous planning, the implementation of appropriate policies, and ongoing monitoring and evaluation.

Carrying Capacity Issues and Excessive Tourism:

The problem of excessive tourism at well-known destinations can result in the deterioration of the natural environment, the loss of cultural traditions, and the straining of the local infrastructure. It is absolutely essential, in order to reduce the negative effects of over-tourism, to put into action strategies that will manage tourist flows and build sustainable carrying capacities.

Insufficient Knowledge, Awareness, and Education:

A lack of sustainable tourism practices awareness and understanding among travelers, businesses, and local communities can be a barrier to the adoption of responsible behaviors and initiatives. The promotion of a culture of sustainability requires the implementation of educational initiatives and training programs.

Problems arising from politics and regulations:

It is possible for the adoption of environmentally responsible tourist practices to be hampered by policies, regulatory frameworks, and enforcement mechanisms that are inconsistent or insufficient. It is absolutely necessary, in order to conquer these obstacles, to align the priorities of the government with the aims of sustainable development.

The concept of sustainable tourism is not only a fad; rather, it refers to a way of traveling that is fundamentally aligned with the protection of our planet, our cultural legacy, and the prosperity of the communities that are visited. Because the tourism industry all over the world is expanding at such a rapid rate, sustainable business practices are no longer a desirable choice but rather a need for the industry's continued success in the long run. Travelers, local businesses, and those in charge of managing tourist destinations may all play a part in making tourism a positive force in the world by adhering to the tenets of sustainable tourism and so ensuring that it will continue to foster the preservation of sociocultural traditions, natural habitats, and economic growth. Even if the path to sustainable tourism may be difficult to navigate, the final destination is a world in which travel and tourism are beneficial to all parties involved, from the natural world to the communities who warmly welcome tourists.

4.1 Principles of Sustainable Tourism

The practice of sustainable tourism is based on a framework that strikes a balance between the protection of natural and cultural resources, the facilitation of economic growth, and the empowerment of the people that are directly affected by tourism. By following to a set of fundamental principles, the tourism sector may reduce the negative effects it has on the environment, safeguard cultural assets, and guarantee that the communities that are host to tourists benefit from the presence of tourists. Within the context of this in-depth investigation, we will investigate the fundamental tenets of sustainable tourism, placing particular emphasis on the significance of ethical business operations, conservation activities, and community involvement. The travel and leisure business can create a more sustainable and ethical approach to travel and leisure by first comprehending and then putting into practice these fundamental ideas.

1. **Activities Related to the Protection and Preservation of the Environment**

   The Maintenance of Biological Variety:

   The maintenance of biological variety and the integrity of natural ecosystems is given considerable weight in the practice of sustainable tourism. It is possible for the tourism sector to have less of an effect on the natural environment provided ethical wildlife watching procedures are put into place, vulnerable ecosystems are preserved, and endangered species are safeguarded.

   Reduction of One's Carbon Footprint

   It is essential to the fight against climate change to cut down on the carbon footprint left by tourism activities. Sustainable tourism encourages the adoption of energy-saving techniques, the use of renewable energy sources, and the utilization of environmentally friendly modes of transportation in order to reduce the amount of greenhouse gases emitted and to advance environmental sustainability.

   The Administration of Waste and Recycling:

   It is necessary to have efficient waste management and recycling programs in place in order to keep tourist locations clean and to reduce the amount of pollution that occurs there. The tourism industry can make a contribution to the preservation of natural habitats by educating visitors and companies about the importance of environmentally responsible garbage disposal and recycling practices.

   The Practice of Conserving Water:

   Sustainable tourism places an emphasis on the significance of water conservation and the utilization of water resources in a responsible manner. The sustainability of tourism destinations is improved, in particular in areas that are water-scarce, by putting

into action water-saving efforts, promoting technology that are water-efficient, and raising awareness about the significance of the preservation of water resources.

2. **Sociocultural Preserving and Admiration of Traditions**

   A Respect for the Traditions and Cultures of the Area:
   Respecting and protecting the distinctive cultures and customs of the communities that are visited as part of responsible tourism is essential. It is important for tourists and tourism enterprises to get involved in cultural exchange programs, show support for local artisans and craftsmen, and take part in cultural events in a way that is respectful of the norms and traditions practiced by the community to which they are traveling.

   Empowerment of Neighborhoods and Community Groups:
   Through the provision of economic possibilities, the promotion of community-based tourism projects, and the facilitation of community participation in decision-making processes that affect the tourism industry, sustainable tourism works toward the goal of empowering the local communities that it visits. It is possible for the tourism sector to ensure that the advantages of tourism are distributed fairly among members of the community if it involves local inhabitants in the process of tourism development.

   The Maintenance of the Cultural Heritage:
   It is essential for the continued existence of a destination's cultural identity that historical sites, monuments, and traditional architecture be preserved. Through the implementation of responsible tourist practices that safeguard historical landmarks, museums, and cultural events, sustainable tourism contributes to the preservation of the world's diverse cultural heritage.

   Education and Intercultural Communication:
   It is possible to create mutual understanding, respect, and appreciation by encouraging cultural interaction and educational activities between visitors and the communities to which they are traveling. The socio-cultural experience is improved for both

tourists and the communities that host them as a result of sustainable tourism's promotion of learning about other cultures, increased cultural awareness, and the exchange of languages.

3. **The Viability of the Economic Model and the Fair Distribution of Benefits**

   Development of the Community's Economy:

   The creation of employment opportunities, the support of small enterprises, and the promotion of the purchase of locally produced goods and services are all ways in which sustainable tourism helps to contribute to the economic growth of local communities. The tourism industry has the potential to drive economic growth while simultaneously reducing its reliance on sources of income from the outside world if local enterprises are brought into the supply chain.

   The distribution of revenues and the prevention of revenue loss:

   It is vital, in order to foster economic sustainability, to make certain that the cash generated by tourism is divided fairly among the local stakeholders. These stakeholders include small business owners, entrepreneurs, and community members. Through the encouragement of local ownership of tourism firms and the reinvestment of earnings into the local economy, sustainable tourism works to reduce the amount of revenue that is lost as a result of revenue leakage.

   Building People's Capacity and Developing Their Skills:

   Increasing local residents' capacity to find work and fostering an entrepreneurial spirit within the

   tourism industry can be accomplished by making investments in programs that foster capacity building and skill development. The tourist industry has the ability to produce a competent labor force that is capable of addressing the ever-changing demands of the industry if it makes chances for training and education available to its employees.

Diversification of Tourism and Participation in Community Life:

It may be possible to more equitably divide the economic benefits of tourism by expanding the range of products and services offered by the tourism industry beyond the models of mass tourism and by incorporating the communities directly in the creation of niche tourism goods and services. The tourist sector has the potential to develop a more inclusive and sustainable tourism economy by putting more emphasis on community-based tourism projects, cultural events, and environmentally responsible tourism practices.

4. **Awareness and Responsible Conduct on the Part of Visitors Best Practices for Responsible Travel:**

It is vital to encourage responsible travel activities among tourists in order to promote sustainable tourism. These practices include showing respect for local customs and traditions, reducing the amount of garbage generated, and supporting local businesses. The tourism sector can help promote a culture of responsible tourist behavior among travelers if more people are aware of the environmental and socio-cultural implications of tourism and are educated about those impacts.

Ethical shopping and support of the local economy:

A significant factor that helps to the long-term economic viability of tourist destinations is the encouragement of ethical consumption patterns among visitors, as well as patronage of locally owned companies, artists, and farmers. In order to lessen the impact that tourism has on the surrounding environment, sustainable tourism places an emphasis on the significance of purchasing goods that are created locally, consuming food that is acquired in a sustainable manner, and using as little single-use plastic as possible.

Education for the Environment and a Consciousness of the Need to Conserve:

It is essential, in order to cultivate a sense of environmental stewardship among visitors, to educate tourists about the significance of preserving the environment, protecting biodiversity, and engaging in tourism practices that are environmentally responsible. The travel and tourism business has the potential to foster a more in-depth comprehension of the natural environment and the critical importance of its protection by hosting educational programs, guided nature excursions, and workshop events on conservation.

Respectful interaction and sensitivity to different cultures:

It is vital, in order to generate positive cross-cultural encounters, to promote cultural sensitivity among tourists and to encourage polite contact between tourists and the local people. The tourism sector may assist tourists in navigating varied cultural situations and engaging with local citizens in a manner that is polite and meaningful by offering cultural orientation workshops, language training, and cultural etiquette guidelines.

5. **The Management and Planning of Vacation Destinations**

Infrastructure and Planning for a Sustainable Future:

The practice of sustainable tourism promotes destination management that places an emphasis on the creation of environmentally friendly infrastructure, amenities that are efficient in their use of energy, and responsible land use planning. The tourism sector can establish destinations that have a smaller negative impact on the surrounding environment if it places a higher emphasis on sustainable development principles.

Reduce the Impact of Overtourism:

A significant obstacle to environmentally responsible tourism is the phenomenon known as "overtourism," which is exemplified by an excessive number of tourists at well-known tourist locations. It is possible for the tourism sector to use techniques such as visitor quotas, timed admission tickets, and crowd control measures in order to combat the negative effects of overtourism and maintain the ecological and cultural sustainability of popular tourist destinations.

Participation of the Community in Planning:

When local communities are involved in the design and management of tourism sites, it guarantees that the needs and concerns of those communities are taken into consideration. The tourist sector may develop a collaborative approach to destination management by routinely undertaking consultations, surveys, and other community involvement efforts.

Framework for Regulatory Compliance and Administration:

It is absolutely necessary to have both efficient regulatory frameworks and severe enforcement mechanisms in place in order to guarantee the implementation of sustainable tourism practices. The tourist industry may hold stakeholders accountable for their activities and limit the negative impact of tourism by enacting policies and laws that promote responsible tourism behavior. These policies and regulations can be found here.

The concept of sustainable tourism is not limited to a single guiding principle; rather, it refers to an approach that takes into account a variety of factors, including economic viability, sociocultural preservation, environmental protection, and responsible behavior on the part of tourists. By adhering to these fundamental values, the tourist sector has the potential to turn itself into a force for good, making a contribution to the protection of natural and cultural resources, the empowerment of local communities, and the equal distribution of economic gains. The concept of sustainable tourism is more than just a goal; rather, it is a commitment to the creation of travel experiences that honor the diversity of the globe, preserve its ecosystems, and improve the lives of its people.

The tenets of sustainable tourism open the way for a more moral and accountable approach to travel and leisure, an approach that can aid in the preservation of the planet while also providing advantages to the people who make that world their home.

4.2 Balancing Economic Growth with Environmental Conservation

There has never been a time when the need to strike a balance between the expansion of the economy and the protection of the natural world was more important than it is now in the face of mounting environmental issues and growing concerns about climate change. The maintenance of this precarious equilibrium is not only doable, but essential to the health of our planet throughout the course of many future generations. During this in-depth investigation, we will delve into the intricate dynamic that exists between the promotion of economic growth and the protection of the environment. We will investigate the difficulties, possibilities, and approaches that can be utilized to bring these ostensibly competing forces into harmony.

1. **The Predicament of Balancing Economic Development and Environmental Protection**
   The Role of Economic Growth as a Motivating Factor:
   The expansion of a nation's economy is frequently regarded as a crucial sign of that nation's development and prosperity. It propels the production of new jobs, higher salaries, higher living standards, and an overall improvement in the well-being of society. Innovation and technical improvement are both fueled by it, which in turn propels forward movement in a variety of fields, including healthcare, education, and the expansion of physical infrastructure.
   The Importance of Preserving the Environment as a Necessity
   At the same time, the environment serves as the basis for all activities related to economics and the continued existence of humans. Ecosystems are responsible for the provision of essential services such as the cleansing of air and water and the maintenance of rich soil. Agriculture and food security are both helped along by biodiversity. The prevention of climate change, the lessening of pollution, and the maintenance of the earth's natural splendor are all

made possible via the practice of environmental conservation.

The Disagreement:

The contention stems from the historically prevalent view that increased economic progress inexorably results in deterioration of the surrounding natural environment. The rapid spread of urbanization, industrialization, and the extraction of resources have frequently come at the expense of the planet's ecosystems and its biodiversity. The tension that exists between fostering economic expansion and protecting natural resources has accelerated the need for a strategy that strikes a better balance.

2. **The Crucial Role of Sustainable Development in Today's World**

The Meaning Behind the Term "Sustainable Development"

This conundrum gave rise to the concept of sustainable development, which places an emphasis on the requirement to strike a balance between economic expansion, social justice, and environmental protection. This strategy acknowledges that ecological, economic, and social objectives are interwoven, and that in order to achieve long-term success, these objectives need to be balanced.

Principles Crucial to the Achieving of Sustainable Development

1. **Economic Efficiency:** Promoting the effective use of resources while reducing waste as much as possible.
2. **Social Equity:** Ensuring that the benefits of economic progress are dispersed fairly across all aspects of society; this refers to the concept of social equity.
3. **Environmental Stewardship:** The act of conserving natural resources as well as ecosystems and biodiversity through actions that are socially and environmentally responsible.

An Agenda for Sustainable Development Based on the Year 2030:

The 2030 Agenda of the United Nations, which includes 17 Sustainable Development Goals (SDGs), is a global framework for striking a balance between economic expansion and the preservation of the natural environment. The challenges of poverty, hunger, health, education, and the use of clean energy, as well as life on land and in the ocean, are all addressed by these goals. They highlight the link of economic goals and environmental goals as a central theme.

III. Possibilities for Establishing Harmony

Technologies that are good for the environment and clean energy:

Both economic expansion and the preservation of the natural environment can be promoted by formulating economic growth strategies that incorporate environmentally friendly technologies and sources of clean energy. Opportunities for expansion that do not need excessive use of resources can be found through the use of sustainable agricultural techniques, energy-efficient technologies, and renewable sources of energy.

Economy Based on Circulation:

The model of a circular economy places an emphasis on both the efficient use of resources and the minimization of waste. It offers a technique to improve economic activity while conserving resources and decreasing pollution by encouraging recycling, reuse, and the reduction of material waste.

Ecotourism and other forms of tourism based on nature

The appreciation of natural settings, wildlife, and ecosystems can be turned into a lucrative industry through ecotourism and nature-based tourism. Opportunities for economic growth are provided by these industries, which also encourage the preservation of natural resources.

Agriculture and forestry with minimal environmental impact:

The goals of sustainable agriculture and agroforestry methods are to raise agricultural production while simultaneously preserving biodiversity, soil, and water resources. These practices boost economic growth while reducing the negative effects that agriculture has on the surrounding environment.

IV. Obstacles and Potential Compromises

Gains in the Short Term vs Sustainability in the Long Term:

The tendency to pursue short-term benefits at the price of long-term sustainability is one of the primary obstacles that must be overcome in order to strike a healthy balance between economic expansion and preservation of the natural environment. Because of political and economic pressures, immediate economic rewards are frequently prioritized, which may put the health of the environment and the well-being of future generations at risk.

Pollution and the Exhaustion of Resources:

Rapid economic growth is frequently accompanied by both the depletion of resources and the contamination of the environment. The extraction of non-sustainable resources, the clearing of forests, and the release of pollutants all contribute to the destruction of the ecosystem. In order to strike a healthy balance between these behaviors and growth, tougher laws and enforcement measures are required.

Unequal Distribution of Income:

The distribution of wealth does not necessarily become more egalitarian as an economy grows. When there is income disparity, some groups may receive a disproportionate amount of benefits from economic development, while other groups, frequently vulnerable populations, face the price of the development in terms of the environment and society.

The Impact of Globalization on Supply Chains

Because of the increasing internationalization of supply chains, it is now more difficult to track the environmental impact of individual items. While economic expansion is seen in every corner of the world, the negative effects on the environment are frequently localized to certain areas, which can make it more difficult to achieve conservation goals.

V. Methods for Achieving an Optimal State of Balance

Frameworks for Regulatory Compliance:

It is absolutely necessary to have regulatory frameworks that work effectively to uphold environmental standards and encourage responsible behavior. When it comes to formulating and enacting policies that direct economic activities toward sustainability, governments have the potential to play a crucial role.

Encouragements and financial aid:

Businesses can be encouraged to adopt environmentally friendly procedures and invest in clean technology through the use of incentives, tax breaks, and subsidies. These economic incentives offer monetary assistance to projects that are beneficial to the environment.

CSR stands for "corporate social responsibility"

Adopting CSR activities that promote environmental conservation in addition to profit can be one way for businesses to contribute to the process of striking a balance. Now more than ever, businesses understand how critical it is to balance economic expansion with environmental responsibility.

Education and a Consciousness of the Facts:

It is absolutely necessary to educate people about the link of economic growth and environmental preservation and to raise public awareness of this interdependence. Citizens who are well-informed have the ability to demand environmentally responsible policies and practices from both their government and the business sector.

The task of striking a balance between expanding the economy and protecting the environment is a complex but necessary one. In a time when the climate is changing and we are losing biodiversity, maintaining this equilibrium is crucial to our future. There are many obstacles to overcome, but sustainable development models, international agendas, and technology breakthroughs give us hope for a future in which growth and conservation can live in a peaceful manner. The essential changes can be catalyzed by the implementation of effective rules, economic incentives, and enhanced awareness.

The examples that have been established by nations and areas that have successfully adopted this strategy highlight the possibility of achieving economic prosperity while also safeguarding our planet for the generations that will come after us. Finding a happy medium between expanding the economy and protecting the natural world is not simply a worthy goal; it is also an important obligation we have for the here and now as well as the legacy we intend to pass on to future generations.

4.3 Community Engagement in Sustainable Tourism

Participation in the local community is essential to the development of sustainable tourism. It ensures that the economic, social, and environmental advantages of tourism are spread fairly and entails the active participation of local people in the development of tourism. In this in-depth study, we investigate the significance of community participation in sustainable tourism, focusing on its fundamental principles, the most effective approaches, the difficulties that it faces, and the part it plays in the protection of cultural heritage, the preservation of the environment, and the promotion of economic well-being.

1. **The Importance of Involvement in Local Communities for Ecologically Responsible Tourism**
   Providing Support to the Neighborhoods:
   The empowerment of local residents to participate in and benefit from tourism development is facilitated through community engagement in sustainable tourism. It involves decision-making processes that take into consideration the requirements and goals of the community as a whole.
   Taking Care of Our Cultural Heritage:
   Communities on a local level frequently serve as the stewards of their own areas' distinct cultural history. Their participation in the tourism industry assures that these cultural assets will be preserved and promoted for future generations. Visitors are provided with genuine cultural experiences while also contributing to the

preservation of local customs and traditions.

The Protection of the Environment:

The participation of local communities in initiatives to conserve the environment contributes to the protection of natural resources and ecosystems. When communities have a vested interest in the preservation of their surroundings, it elevates the issue to the level of a communal responsibility that extends beyond the short-term financial benefits of tourism.

Prosperity in Financial Aspects:

Tourism has the potential to spur economic growth in local communities by fostering the development of new job possibilities, assisting the expansion of existing small enterprises, and bringing in new money. Participation in community life guarantees that these economic benefits are dispersed equitably among local individuals.

2. **Core Values of Community Involvement in Environmentally Responsible Tourism**

The inclusiveness of:

It is important that every person of the community, regardless of age, gender, or socioeconomic standing, has the chance to take part in the development of tourism in the community. The inclusion of a variety of perspectives guarantees that they will be heard.

Openness and honesty:

Trust among community members can be increased through transparent decision-making processes and the distribution of resources. Residents of the area need to be aware of both the positive and negative aspects of tourism.

A Division of the Rewards:

It is only fair that local communities receive a portion of the financial benefits that tourism provides. This can be accomplished through the establishment of revenue-sharing systems, the promotion of locally owned and operated businesses, and the creation of local jobs.

Construction of Capabilities:

Training and education programs should be provided in order to increase the skills and capabilities of community members. This will enable community members to actively participate in activities and management that are relevant to tourism.

3. **Examples of Exemplary Practices Regarding Community Involvement**

Enterprises Founded on the Principle of Community Tourism:

Homestays, local tour guides, and artisan cooperatives are all examples of community-based tourist firms that might benefit from financial support and promotion. This helps to guarantee that the economic benefits of tourism are distributed evenly across the community.

Making Decisions Through Participation:

A sense of ownership and accountability can be fostered among local residents by including them in decision-making processes regarding the growth of tourism, the use of land, and the preservation of environmental resources.

Initiatives for the Cultural Preservation of

Investing in cultural preservation efforts, such as language revitalization, traditional arts, and heritage preservation, helps to promote the community's cultural identity and improves the experience that tourists have when they visit the area.

Responsible management of the environment

The participation of local communities in environmental conservation efforts, such as reforestation, garbage management, and wildlife protection, is one way to contribute to the preservation of the natural resources that are attractive to tourists.

Education and a Consciousness of the Facts:

It is possible to encourage cultural knowledge, responsible behavior, and a respect of local customs by delivering education and awareness programs to tourists as well as residents of the local community.

4. **Obstacles Facing Participation in the Community**

Disproportion of Power:
Ineffective community participation can be a result of power inequalities, which is especially problematic in situations when tourism businesses and government organizations hold greater influence than local populations. It is important to make an effort to ensure that decision-making is both inclusive and participatory in nature.

Restricted Access to Resources:
The limited resources available in rural and distant communities can make it difficult for those communities to fully participate in the development of tourism. Building up one's capabilities and having access to finance are both crucial components in overcoming these obstacles.

Appropriation de la culture:
Travel and tourism have been linked to instances of cultural appropriation, which occurs when aspects of one culture are commercialized and distorted for the sake of making a profit.

It is essential to create a balance between sharing one's culture and ensuring that its originality is maintained.

Excessive Tourism:
An excessive amount of tourists can put a burden on a community's resources and infrastructure, which can lead to environmental degradation and have a negative influence on the locals' day-to-day existence. The effective management of tourist flows is essential to the mitigation of this problem.

Participation in local activities is an essential component of tourism that has far-reaching positive effects on the environment. When local communities are actively involved in the development of tourism, they become guardians of their cultural heritage and natural surroundings, guaranteeing that these aspects of their environment will be preserved for future generations. The economic gains brought about by tourism are shared fairly among the locals, which ultimately helps to improve their standard of living. Despite the fact that there are hurdles, there are also effective solutions and best practices that can alleviate these challenges, thereby producing a win-win scenario in which tourism benefits the community and the community helps to better the experience of tourists. Engaging with the local community is not just one of the tenets of sustainable tourism; it is also essential to the industry's development and the preservation of the planet's myriad ecosystems and cultural traditions.

Chapter 5

Tourism and Cultural Preservation

Both the tourism industry and the preservation of cultural traditions are essential to the modern world. As a result of tourism's continued growth and expansion across the globe, the protection of cultural heritage frequently faces a number of opportunities as well as obstacles. While tourism can be beneficial to the economy and can encourage cultural interaction, it also has the potential to threaten important cultural monuments and customs. It is imperative that a balance be found between the two in order to guarantee that future generations will be able to appreciate and gain knowledge from the complex tapestry that is human history and culture. During this in-depth investigation, we will delve into the complex relationship that exists between tourism and the preservation of cultural traditions. We will investigate the potential advantages and disadvantages of this relationship, as well as investigate case studies from all over the world and provide solutions for maintaining peaceful coexistence.

1. The Intersection of Tourism and the Protection of Cultural Objects

1.1. The Favorable Effects of Tourism on the Conservation of Cultural Property

It is common practice to consider tourism as a two-edged sword, one that is both capable of destroying cultural heritage and of protecting it. While it is necessary to recognize the difficulties and dangers, it is as essential to have an understanding of the good effects that tourism may have on the maintenance of cultural traditions.

1.1.1. Benefits to the Economy Tourism has the potential to bring large revenue into local communities. This money has the potential to be put back into initiatives to preserve cultural heritage. The collection of entrance fees, the provision of guided tours, and the marketing and sale of regionally produced goods and wares are all potential revenue sources for the preservation of cultural heritage.

1.1.2. Heightened Awareness The influx of tourists can heighten one's awareness of the cultural legacy of a particular location. When people travel there, both domestically and internationally, they have the potential to become advocates for the preservation of local culture if they recognize the importance of the culture there.

1.1.3. Cultural interaction Tourism acts as a catalyst for cultural interaction, which in turn promotes mutual appreciation and comprehension between other communities. On a global scale, this might lead to a sense of shared responsibility for the preservation of cultural assets.

1.1.4. Developments in Technology Tourism is frequently the primary impetus for the need to enhance infrastructure and technology, both of which have the potential to be utilized in the conservation of cultural assets. Because of the increased interest in tourism, preservation techniques have evolved, including digitization and scanning in three dimensions.

1.2 The Difficulties and Dangers Involved

It is a difficult effort to strike a balance between the benefits of tourism and the problems and dangers that it poses.

1.2.1. Overcrowding is a problem that can affect popular tourist places, and it can result in physical damage to cultural assets, an increase in pollution, and an overall decrease in the quality of the experience that visitors have.

1.2.2. Commercialization The need for profit can lead to commercialization, which is when cultural sites become unduly commercialized and lose their authenticity, which diminishes the value of their cultural status.

1.2.3. Loss of Traditions The influx of tourists can have an effect on local customs and ways of life, leading to a standardization of culture and a decrease in the number of traditional practices.

1.2.4. Irresponsible Behavior: Some tourists engage in irresponsible behavior, such as littering, leaving graffiti, or stealing, which can result in damage being done to cultural sites and objects.

2. **Methodologies for Maintaining Peaceful Coexistence**

    2.1. Awareness and Educational Initiatives

    It is of the utmost importance to raise awareness among tourists and the local community. The cultural significance of the locations that tourists visit ought to be explained to those tourists, and the communities that host tourists ought to have an understanding of both the financial rewards and the responsibilities that come along with tourism.

    2.2. Access That Is Regulated

    It is possible to prevent congestion at cultural sites and decrease the impact on both the infrastructure and the environment by setting a maximum number of visitors per day. This strategy has been used effectively in the preservation of historical sites such as Machu Picchu and Angkor Wat.

    2.3. Tourism That Is Sustainable

    The practice of promoting sustainable tourism practices entails reducing tourism's negative influence on the environment, bolstering local economies, and protecting cultural heritage. This can be accomplished through the use of environmentally friendly modes of transportation, responsible lodging, and active participation in the community at large.

2.4 Science, Engineering, and New Product Development

Utilizing technology, such as methods of digital preservation, is one way to assist in the preservation of cultural heritage. The creation of virtual experiences, which can lessen the amount of physical wear and tear on places, can be accomplished through the use of digitization, 3D scanning, and augmented reality.

2.5. Participation in the Community

It is essential that local communities be involved in the administration of tourism. When citizens of a community have a financial interest in tourism, they are more likely to preserve their cultural traditions and assure the industry's continued viability over the long run.

2.6. Legal Structures and Regulatory Frameworks

It is necessary to enact laws and regulations that protect cultural heritage and to ensure that they are followed. It is important for national governments and international organizations to collaborate on the development of legal frameworks that would both protect history and encourage tourism.

2.7. Management Strategies for Cultural Tourism Plans

It is absolutely necessary to devise comprehensive management plans for cultural tourism that strike a balance between tourism and preservation. These preparations ought to take into account the one-of-a-kind requirements and difficulties presented by each trip.

2.8 International Cooperation and Coordination

Cooperation on a global scale is absolutely necessary in order to preserve our common cultural legacy. Cross-border preservation of cultural places is possible through cooperative efforts between nations, international organizations, and non-governmental organizations (NGOs).

3. Future Difficulties and Potential Opportunities

3.1. Excessive Tourism

The issue of overtourism is still a big one. The management of the negative effects that mass tourism has on cultural assets will need the development of new solutions, such as guiding tourists to locations that are less often frequented or staggering the hours at which they can visit.

3.2. The Changing Climate

The effects of climate change, such as rising sea levels, increasingly severe weather, and shifting climatic conditions, pose a threat to cultural monuments. A major worry is finding ways to adapt to these difficulties while also conserving heritage from the effects of climate change.

3.3. Tourism Virtual (Online)

The development of technologies such as virtual reality and augmented reality has made it possible for tourists to experience a place's cultural legacy even while they are physically absent. This can reduce the strain that is placed on physical sites while still providing visitors with a comprehensive cultural encounter.

3.4. The Promotion of Cultural Efforts

The act of preserving culture should not be restricted to merely preserving the way things are currently. It may also involve reviving customs and rituals that have become extinct or have become less prevalent over the course of time. A revitalized interest in the culture of a place is one way in which tourism can contribute to the solution of this problem.

3.5. Certification for Environmentally Responsible Tourism

The establishment of sustainable tourism certification schemes and the broad adoption of these programs can assist in directing tourists toward more responsible options and push the industry to adopt environmentally friendly practices.

3.6 Tourism Following an Epidemic

The pandemic caused by the COVID-19 virus has had a substantial effect on the tourism industry. As it begins to heal, there will be an opportunity to rebuild in a manner that is more responsible and sustainable, with an emphasis on the preservation of cultural traditions.

Both tourism and the preservation of cultural traditions are crucial components of today's world, and it is imperative that the two be brought into harmony with one another. Tourism can be beneficial to the economy and promote cultural interaction, but it also presents obstacles to the conservation of cultural heritage. We are able to ensure that tourism and cultural preservation can coexist if we have an awareness of the beneficial impacts tourism may have, as well as the obstacles and hazards that are involved with tourism, we investigate case studies from across the world, and we adopt sustainable plans. As we move forward, it is essential that we maintain our capacity for adaptation and innovation in order to face the ever-evolving challenges and possibilities that lie ahead. This will help to ensure that the rich tapestry of human history and culture is preserved for future generations to enjoy and learn from.

5.1 The Intersection of Tourism and Culture

Culture and tourism have a complex and intertwined relationship, which creates an intersection at which the singularity of different cultures collides with the inquiry and curiosity of tourists. This junction is a dynamic venue that showcases the history, traditions, and customs of a location to tourists who are looking to immerse themselves in a variety of cultural experiences. Within this comprehensive relationship, the influences of tourism on culture and vice versa are enormous, resulting to a complex tapestry of global trade. This relationship also has many other facets. It is essential to have an understanding of this junction in order to cultivate tourist practices that are sustainable and courteous while also supporting the preservation and appreciation of varied cultures all around the world.

The Role of Tourism in Fostering Intercultural Communication

Tourism, at its foundation, serves as a catalyst for cultural exchange. It enables individuals to experience and appreciate the diversity of human civilizations by providing them with the

opportunity to travel to other countries. This interaction helps to create an awareness across cultures as well as tolerance and respect for other ways of life and traditions. As a result of their contacts with the local people, tourists receive insights into the cultural fabric of a location, which contributes to a greater understanding of the world as a whole and a deeper appreciation of the intricacies of different cultures.

The locations of cultural heritage, museums, festivals, and culinary experiences are frequently the focal points of this interchange. They serve as bridges that connect tourists to the rich history, art, and customs of a particular location.

Through the promotion of cultural tourism, tourists are encouraged to partake in genuine experiences while they are away, such as by taking part in local festivals, learning about traditional crafts, or delighting in regional food. This results in a stronger connection with the culture of the destination.

In addition, the interaction of people from different cultures brought about by tourism frequently leads to the development of novel cultural hybrids. These cultural hybrids result in the production of new art forms, cuisines, and traditions that exemplify the essence of cultural diversity and shared human experiences.

Maintaining One's Cultural Identities Despite the Growth of Tourism

Travel and tourism have the potential to not only foster cultural interchange but also present obstacles to the protection of cultural identities. It is possible that the commercialization and commodification of cultural practices would occur unintentionally as a result of an increase in the number of tourists visiting increasingly popular areas. It is possible that local populations will adjust their cultural traditions in order to satisfy the needs of tourists, which will result in a loss of authenticity in their legacy. In addition, the rapid development of infrastructure for tourism can encroach upon historical sites and natural landscapes, posing a risk to the authenticity of cultural landmarks.

Nevertheless, the protection of cultural identity in the face of increased tourism can be accomplished by the concerted promotion of tourism activities that are environmentally responsible. It is possible to maintain traditional norms and principles when local communities are given the authority and the opportunity to take an active role in the administration of tourism. It is possible to assist in the preservation of the originality and integrity of cultural heritage sites by enforcing responsible tourism behavior and implementing policies that limit the exploitation of cultural practices for the purpose of commercial gain.

Increasing Travelers' Awareness of, and Respect for, Different Cultures

Within the framework of the interaction of culture and tourism, it is essential to encourage cultural sensitivity and respect among those who are traveling. Fostering an environment of mutual understanding and appreciation can be accomplished by encouraging tourists to accept cultural diversity and respect local customs and traditions. Education programs that provide historical and cultural background to tourists before they travel as well as while they are there can help to a more meaningful and respectful interaction with the culture of the area where they are traveling.

In addition, promoting responsible tourism practices such as reducing environmental impact, protecting sacred places, and supporting local artists and businesses can help to cultivate a partnership that is mutually beneficial to both cultures and tourism. Homestays, cultural workshops, and other community-based tourism initiatives can help tourists gain a deeper understanding of the significance of preserving cultural heritage for future generations if they are engaged in immersive cultural experiences that prioritize authentic interactions with local communities.

Finding a Middle Ground Between Economic Growth and Cultural Persistence

The interaction of tourism and culture calls for a difficult balancing act between the expansion of the economy and the preservation of cultural traditions. Even if tourism has the potential to jumpstart economic growth and improve the standard of living of local people, it is of the utmost importance to guarantee that this expansion is both sustainable and does not come at the expense of the region's cultural authenticity.

It is possible to cultivate a partnership that is mutually beneficial for tourism and the local economy by putting into action tourist programs that are driven by the local community and that reinvest a percentage of their revenue in the protection and dissemination of cultural traditions. It is possible to divide the economic advantages of tourism more fairly by encouraging the diversification of tourism offers beyond mainstream attractions and promoting experiences that are off the beaten path. This can also help reduce the burden that is placed on popular tourist locations.

Advancing Eco-Friendly Tourism Policies and Procedures

When it comes to the convergence of tourism and culture, sustainable tourism practices play a key role, helping to the long-term preservation of cultural assets in the process. It is possible to lessen the impact of tourism on cultural sites and the surroundings around them by embracing practices that are kind to the environment. Some of these practices include encouraging eco-friendly modes of transportation, cutting down on waste made of plastic, and providing support for sustainable housing options.

It is possible to assure the successful implementation of sustainable tourism policies by incorporating cultural preservation into destination management plans and working in collaboration with local stakeholders, non-governmental organizations, and governmental entities. Destinations are able to protect their one-of-a-kind cultural heritage while also cultivating a flourishing and environmentally responsible tourism business if they incorporate the concepts of cultural preservation into the laws that guide tourism development.

The junction of tourism and culture exemplifies a dynamic and ever-evolving interaction. This relationship is characterized by the interchange of knowledge, customs, and experiences. It is crucial for promoting sustainable tourism practices and conserving the diversity of global cultures to acknowledge the significance of this nexus in creating cross-cultural understanding and respect. We can ensure that the intersection of tourism and culture continues to be a space for meaningful global exchange by fostering a mutual respect for cultural heritage, empowering local communities, and promoting responsible tourism behavior. This will help us to create a world in which cultural diversity is celebrated and preserved for future generations.

5.2 Cultural Attractions and Tourism

The vivid fabric of a destination's tradition, history, and artistic expression is made up of the destination's cultural attractions. These attractions include a diverse assortment of aspects, ranging from festivals, culinary traditions, and performances to historical buildings, museums, and art galleries. They offer glimpses into the culture and history of a location, acting as windows that draw tourists in with the promise of one-of-a-kind experiences. Tourists are not just immersed in a world of various traditions, practices, and values when they visit cultural attractions; sightseeing is only one facet of what these destinations have to offer. In the course of this in-depth investigation, we will investigate the value of cultural attractions in tourism, looking closely at the roles that these attractions play in fostering economic growth, cultural preservation, and intercultural understanding.

1. **The Importance of Cultural Attractions to the Travel and Tourism Industry**

   Many places all around the world rely heavily on tourism, and cultural attractions are essential to this industry. Their importance is not limited to the fact that they are merely points of interest; rather, it lies in the multifarious roles they play in forming the tourist sector and improving the quality of travel experiences.

1.1. Primary Driver of the Economy

Attractions of cultural significance make a substantial contribution to the economic growth of destinations. They bring in tourists and bring in cash through the sale of souvenirs, local crafts and cuisine, as well as by the collection of entrance fees and guided tour costs. In addition to that, these attractions help the local economy by increasing demand for services such as hotels, restaurants, transportation, and retail.

1.2. The Protection of Cultural Assets

Many times, the tradition and history of a location are preserved by the cultural attractions that are located there. The invaluable items and data housed in museums and other historical places are carefully protected to ensure their survival for future generations. These attractions play an important part in preserving the cultural character of a region and in communicating that region's history to the rest of the world.

1.3. Understanding Across Different Cultures

Attractions of cultural significance are potent instruments for advancing an appreciate and understanding of other cultures. They give tourists the opportunity to become immersed in cultures, languages, and philosophies that are vastly different from their own. This sharing of knowledge and experiences helps contribute to the development of a global society that recognizes and appreciates the value of diversity.

2. Different Categories of Cultural Tourist Attractions

2.1 The Museums

Relics from other cultures, as well as works of art and historical objects, can be found in museum collections. They provide guests with the opportunity to dig into the history and creative accomplishments of a particular location. Museums are essential components of key cultural destinations all throughout the world, from the Louvre in Paris to the British Museum in London.

2.2. Historical Places and Relics

Travelers can experience life in bygone ages by visiting historical sites such as castles, ancient ruins, and other locations listed on the UNESCO World Heritage List. Not only do places like the Acropolis in Athens, the Great Wall of China, and Machu Picchu in Peru offer glimpses into the past, but they are also among the most recognizable cultural landmarks in the world.

2.3. Festivities and Occasions for Celebration

Festivals, celebrations, and other events of a cultural nature offer a cultural experience that is both dynamic and immersive. Activities such as the Rio Carnival in Brazil, Diwali in India, and the Oktoberfest in Germany provide visitors the opportunity to take part in and see the lively customs of the culture to which they are traveling.

2.4 Museums and Galleries of Art

Painting, sculpture, and even contemporary installations can all be found hanging on the walls of art galleries as examples of how different cultures express themselves creatively via the visual arts. It is well known that the art collections housed in the Louvre Abu Dhabi, the Guggenheim Museum in New York, and the Uffizi Gallery in Florence are among the finest in the world.

2.5 Landmarks of Architectural Design

Architectural landmarks serve as cultural attractions that illustrate the architectural and engineering brilliance of a place. These landmarks are sometimes considered to be "landmarks." Not only are they architectural marvels, but the Taj Mahal in India, the Sydney Opera House in Australia, and the Sagrada Familia in Spain are all iconic structures that represent the countries in which they are located.

2.6. Experiences in the Culinary Arts

Both the culinary traditions and the food itself play a significant role in the cultural attractions. Food markets, culinary workshops, and restaurants all present travelers with opportunities to have an immersive cultural experience. Local cuisine offers a flavorful glimpse into the identity of a society.

3. **The Mutually Beneficial Relationship Between Cultural Attractions and Tourism**

The relationship between tourist destinations and cultural attractions is naturally one of mutual benefit. The preservation and presentation of cultural assets are aided and supported by tourism, which is the primary driver of cultural tourism.

3.1. The Benefits to the Economy

The tourism industry's robust economic performance can be directly attributed to the major contributions made by cultural attractions. These destinations are extremely popular among vacationers, who typically spend money on mementos created in the area, pay admission fees, and take part in guided excursions. The money that is made is then put back into the economy of the area, helping to generate employment and business opportunities in the retail, transportation, and hospitality industries.

3.2. The Protection of Cultural Assets

The history and traditions of a location might be best preserved through its cultural attractions. Treasured objects, important papers, and long-held customs are frequently committed to the care of cultural institutions such as museums, historic sites, and other historical places. The revenues that are created from tourism are used to support various conservation projects, which include the preservation and restoration of cultural assets.

3.3 Improving the Quality of the Travel Experience

The trip experience is given a richer depth of significance when it includes visits to cultural landmarks. They enhance a trip by providing passengers with the opportunity to connect with the local culture, gain an understanding of the history of the area, and see the artistic expressions of the locals. A journey becomes an adventure in culture when one stops at a historical site or museum along the way.

3.4. Intercultural Communication

The promotion of intercultural understanding is significantly aided by the presence of cultural attractions. When vacationers become immersed in the traditions and customs of a particular location, they inadvertently take on the role of unofficial cultural representatives back in their home countries. This sharing of knowledge and comprehension helps to construct bridges between different cultures and leads to the creation of a world that is more tolerant of and rich in diversity.

4. Obstacles Facing the Administration of Cultural Attractions

4.1. Crowding Conditions

Overcrowding is a common problem at popular cultural destinations, which can have a negative impact not only on the quality of the experience that visitors have there but also on the physical condition of the attraction itself. For example, St. Mark's Square in Venice is infamous for its excessive crowding, which has a negative impact on the ancient buildings there.

4.2. Preserving the Status Quo

The protection of historical objects and cultural heritage is an ongoing and difficult endeavor. It is important for historical sites and museums to display their collections, but it is also important for these institutions to keep their holdings safe for future generations. Important problems include climate control, security, and environmental rehabilitation.

4.3. Tourism That Is Sustainable

Concerns about the toll taken on the natural world by tourism continue to mount. Cultural attractions and the tourism sector as a whole need to adopt more environmentally conscious business methods in order to reduce the ecological footprint they leave behind and safeguard the natural environment that surrounds cultural attractions.

4.4 Availability of Access and Inclusion of All

Every tourist, regardless of their physical capabilities, linguistic capabilities, or cultural background, should be able to enjoy cultural sites that make an effort to be open and welcoming to all tourists. Accessibility and information provision in multiple languages can be difficult tasks for many tourist destinations and attractions.

5. **Methods for the Ethical and Environmentally Responsible Administration of Cultural Landmarks**

   5.1. Administration of Guests

   The implementation of tactics for visitor management, such as timed admission tickets, visitor quotas, and crowd control measures, can assist alleviate concerns linked to overcrowding and safeguard the attraction's overall integrity.

   5.2. Protection and Maintenance of the Environment

   It is essential to make investments in various conservation and preservation measures. To ensure the safety of their collections, museums and other historical sites ought to develop all-encompassing preservation plans. These plans must to incorporate temperature control systems, restoration initiatives, and safety precautions.

   5.3. Methods That Are Environmentally Friendly

   Sustainable tourism practices should be used by cultural attractions. These should include environmentally friendly modes of transportation, trash minimization, and renewable energy sources. They are able to make a contribution to the conservation of the natural environment by minimizing the impact that they have on the surrounding ecosystem.

   5.4 The Availability of Access

   Attractions of cultural significance should make every effort to welcome and accommodate guests of diverse backgrounds and abilities. Important initiatives include making accommodations for people with disabilities, providing information in many languages, and ensuring that cultural attractions are welcoming to visitors who come from a variety of different backgrounds.

5.5. Participation in the Community

Participation from the surrounding community is essential to the maintenance of cultural landmarks. A sense of ownership can be fostered in the community by giving locals responsibilities in the operation, upkeep, and marketing of local attractions. This helps to ensure that the community as a whole reaps the benefits of tourism.

6. The Prospects for Cultural Tourist Attractions in the Years Ahead

6.1. Tourism That Is Sustainable

In the years to come, there will be an increased emphasis placed on eco-friendly tourism

activities. To satisfy the desire for more ethical and environmentally conscious vacation activities, cultural attractions will need to make necessary adjustments. This will involve the incorporation of renewable energy sources, the reduction of trash, and the promotion of solutions for mobility with a minimal impact.

6.2. The Transformation of Digital Technology

The use of digital technology will continue to revolutionize the way in which visitors experience cultural landmarks. Innovative new ways for tourists to connect with cultural heritage will be provided in the form of virtual reality, augmented reality, and interactive exhibitions.

6.3. The Enhancement of Cultural Expression

The revitalization and maintenance of customs and rituals that have been practiced for generations will be helped along by cultural attractions. As part of an effort to both celebrate and preserve cultural variety, several cultural attractions will incorporate initiatives to assist regional craftspeople, culinary traditions, and endangered languages.

6.4 The spirit of inclusion

To ensure that all guests, regardless of their abilities or backgrounds, are able to fully connect with the culture and heritage of the destination, cultural attractions will endeavor to become more inclusive and accessible.

6.5. Promotion of Attractions That Are Slightly Off the Beaten Path

The promotion of cultural attractions that are located away from the typical tourist routes is going to pick up steam as overcrowding and overtourism become increasingly significant concerns. Because of this, tourists will be encouraged to visit places and areas that are not as well known, which will result in a more equitable distribution of the advantages of tourism.

Tourists are drawn to cultural attractions because they provide them the chance to learn about a location's rich history, cultural traditions, and artistic expressions. These attractions are the lifeblood of the tourism industry. They act as economic engines, watchdogs for the preservation of cultural traditions, and bridges to greater understanding between different cultures. It is essential that cultural attractions be managed in a sustainable manner in order to ensure that they continue to make a positive contribution to the tourism sector while also protecting the cultural legacy that they represent.

As the travel and tourism sector continues to develop, cultural attractions will continue to play an essential part in fostering intercultural dialogue, appreciation, and understanding on a worldwide scale. They are priceless gems for tourists who are looking to connect with the various cultures that are found all over the world because of their ability to both stimulate discovery and commemorate heritage. This makes them appealing to tourists for an extended period of time.

5.3 Protecting and Promoting Local Cultures

For the human experience to continue to be as diverse and varied as it has been throughout history, it is essential that local cultures be preserved and promoted. Local cultures are the keepers of one-of-a-kind customs, linguistic varieties, artistic expressions, and ways of life that have developed over the course of centuries. Not only are these cultural expressions valuable in and of themselves, but they also add to the cultural heritage of the entire world. Protecting and promoting local cultures is an urgent necessity in a society characterized by globalization and the ever-expanding reach of mass media. This is necessary to assure the local cultures' continuous existence and continued enrichment. This article discusses the significance of preserving and honoring local cultures, as well as the difficulties those cultures confront and the methods that can be used to conserve and advance them.

The Value of Regional Traditions and Cultures

Diversity of cultures: The myriad of human societies is reflected in the richness and variety of the world's indigenous peoples. They cover a vast variety of customs, tenets, and rituals that are meant to reflect the ideas, ideals, and experiences of the communities to which they belong. Understanding the complexities of the human experience requires having a diverse range of cultural perspectives.

The preservation of history is accomplished through the transmission of historical narratives and the collective memory of a people through their respective local cultures. They serve as a live record of past occurrences, hardships, and victories, and they provide a sense of continuity and identity to the community.

Sense of Belonging and Identity: Individuals and communities owe a significant amount of their identities to the local cultures that they were raised in. They give people a sense of belonging and bring people together by connecting them around a common cultural heritage.

The economic and social value of local cultures is often overlooked, although they are important not only from a cultural perspective. They keep local economies afloat by contributing to tourism, providing job opportunities in cultural industries, and maintaining traditional practices in the arts, crafts, and other fields of endeavor.

Threats to the Existence of Local Cultures

The influence of global media and multinational enterprises can have a detrimental effect on local cultures by encouraging attitudes and conventions that are more Westernized, homogenized, or globalized.

Globalization. This can result in the extinction of indigenous languages, cultural practices, and ways of life.

Appropriation of Culture Appropriation of local culture by individuals or corporations from more dominant cultures can lead to the commercialization and misrepresentation of these cultures, frequently without the benefit of the communities that these cultures belong to. This practice is known as cultural appropriation.

The pressures of tourism While tourism can have positive effects on the economy, it also has the potential to present some difficulties. An overabundance of tourists in a given area can have a devastating impact on the local culture, leading to the commercialization and desecration of important heritage sites and cultural practices.

Rapid urbanization can result in the uprooting of indigenous groups and the disappearance of rural cultural practices; both of these outcomes are caused by urbanization. When people relocate to cities, they frequently leave their more conventional ways of life behind.

Techniques for the Preservation and Advancement of Regional Cultures:

Education and Awareness: The cultivation of cultural awareness and appreciation ought to start with the curricular offerings of educational institutions. This involves the education of local history, traditions, and languages, all of which can help inculcate a respect for a variety of cultural backgrounds beginning at a young age.

Help for Artists and artisans Communities of local artists, artisans, and cultural practitioners should get assistance from their respective governments and organizations. This assistance can be provided in the form of funding, training opportunities, and venues where their work can be displayed.

Programs for the Preservation of Cultural Heritage It is important to launch initiatives devoted to the conservation of cultural traditions. This involves the recording of endangered languages, oral histories, and traditional practices that are at danger of being lost.

Participation of Local Communities: It is necessary to encourage local communities to take part in the process of cultural preservation and promotion.

Communities ought to have a voice in the manner in which their culture is presented to the rest of the world and ought to receive a fair part of the advantages that come with cultural tourism.

Promoting responsible tourism is essential if one wishes to guarantee that tourists respect local traditions and make good contributions to the communities in which they visit. This involves educating tourists about local customs, promoting community-based tourism efforts, and applying visitor control measures to reduce congestion. Educating tourists about local customs is an important part of this.

Collaborative Efforts on a Global Scale Both international cooperation and support are required in order to ensure the survival of local cultures. Protecting and promoting cultural diversity can be accomplished through cooperative efforts between states and international organizations.

Preserving Cultures via Digital Technology Local traditions and cultures can be preserved via the use of digital technology. Virtual reality experiences, online cultural exhibitions, and digital archives are all examples of projects that have the potential to serve as platforms for the dissemination of regional culture to an international audience.

Examples of Initiatives That Have Been Successful:

UNESCO recognizes cultural practices and traditions that need to be protected and promoted and has compiled a list of these practices and traditions called the Intangible Cultural Heritage List. A significant number of nations have been able to effectively nominate aspects of their indigenous cultures for inclusion on this list.

Festivals of Culture: Cultural festivals around the world are held to honor regional customs and customaries, and they attract tourists from all over the world. These events have the potential to generate economic benefits while also conserving and fostering cultural customs and traditions.

Community-Based Tourism: In many regions of the world, local communities have recognized the potential of tourism as a tool for sustaining and advancing their cultural traditions. They provide opportunity for tourists to become fully immersed in local traditions, whether they are visiting the indigenous communities of Peru or the tribal villages of India.

Programs to Revitalize Languages: Language is an Essential Element of Local Culture Language is an essential element of local culture.

In order to safeguard the continuation of languages that are in risk of extinction, such as the Maori language in New Zealand, a number of regions have initiated language revitalization programs.

It is essential to our planet's continued vitality and diversity that local cultures be preserved and celebrated in order to ensure their continued existence. Not only are these cultures valuable in and of themselves, but they also provide important contributions to the cultural heritage of the entire world. It is essential to put into action policies that place an emphasis on education, community participation, responsible tourism, and international cooperation if they are to be successful in overcoming the issues they face. A dedication to variety and an acknowledgment of the significance of cultural history as a formative force in the human experience are both embodied in the act of recognizing, protecting, and honoring local cultures.

5.4 The Impact of Cultural Tourism on Local Economies

Economic Growth The act of inviting tourists to a location for the purpose of cultural tourism can help to generate economic growth. Because tourists spend money on things like lodging, food, transportation, and cultural attractions, the economy of the host community benefits from this influx of capital. In many instances, cultural tourists are willing to spend extra money in order to have a genuine experience. As a result, they are valuable contributors to the economy of the area in which they travel.

Job Creation The cultural tourism industry is responsible for the creation of employment possibilities in a wide variety of disciplines.

These employment include those in tourism and hospitality, as well as those in the transportation and food service industries, as well as those in the cultural and creative industries. The demand for highly trained experts in these fields may open up more employment prospects for people who live in the surrounding area.

Growth of Small Businesses Cultural tourism has the potential to be a savior for locally owned and operated companies. The desire for genuine examples of cultural goods is frequently beneficial to regional producers of traditional foods, crafts, and beverages, as well as to local artisans and crafters. This has the potential to foster the growth of a healthy ecosystem of small firms, which will contribute to the diversification of the local economy.

Infrastructure Development: In order to cater to the needs of cultural tourists, regions may need to make investments in the development of infrastructure, such as the construction of new roads and the expansion of existing transportation and cultural facilities. This not only improves the experience that tourists have, but it also helps the local community and contributes to the growth of the economy over the long term.

Preservation of Culture: Cultural tourism frequently fosters the preservation and revivification of local cultural practices, customs, and history. Communities see the significance of their culture as an asset to tourism and take steps to protect it because of this recognition. This, in turn, can entice a greater number of tourists, so creating a positive feedback loop that contributes to economic expansion.

The impact of cultural tourism on a community's economy is frequently described as having a multiplier effect. When tourists spend money on cultural activities, that money stimulates the local economy since it is then employed by local businesses and individuals for a variety of different objectives. Because of this, the initial economic impact may be amplified.

Culture-based tourism can make a positive contribution to sustainable development by encouraging visitors to gain a greater appreciation for the traditions and history of the places they visit. It does this by encouraging habits that are responsible for tourism as well as a long-term commitment to preserving the identity of the region.

To ensure that both the local economy and the culture that is being represented benefit from cultural tourism, however, it is essential to effectively manage this type of tourism. For instance, excessive tourism can have unintended negative effects, such as an increase in population density and the deterioration of natural resources. As a result, destination management and sustainability initiatives are very necessary in order to maximize the economic potential of cultural tourism while also protecting the natural and cultural riches of a place.

Chapter 6

Infrastructure Development and Tourism

The creation of new infrastructure is one of the most important aspects of the tourism business since it forms the basis of a location's capacity to allure visitors, accommodate their needs, and meet their expectations. The quality and accessibility of the infrastructure has a big impact on the experience that a tourist has, and this includes everything from transportation networks to accommodations, attractions, and services. In this in-depth investigation, we dig into the complex relationship that exists between the growth of tourism and the construction of new infrastructure. We will cover the ways in which infrastructure improves the overall experience of tourists, contributes to economic growth, and encourages sustainability, as well as address the problems and potential pitfalls that are associated with it.

1. **The Role of Investment in Physical Infrastructure in Fostering Tourism Development**
   1.1. Transportational Links and Connections
   The success of the tourism industry is directly correlated to the efficiency of its transportation infrastructure. Roads, airports,

railroads, and ports are some of the important components that make it possible for travelers to conveniently access their locations. The establishment and upkeep of these networks may result in an increase in the number of visitors to a location. This is because tourists are more likely to prefer locations that are simple to reach.

1.2. Provision of Housing

It is essential to have a variety of lodging options available in order to attract a wide variety of travelers; these options should include anything from hotels and resorts to hostels and vacation rentals. It is important for a location to have a variety of well-developed lodging options that can accommodate to a variety of guests' interests as well as their financial constraints in order to maintain its broad appeal.

1.3. Locations of Interest and Amenities

The experience that a tourist has will be greatly influenced by things like the natural and cultural attractions, museums, parks, and recreational facilities.

The creation of infrastructure in these regions, such as the construction of visitor centers, interpretation facilities, and walking paths, can improve the experience that tourists have while they are there and encourage them to stay for longer periods of time.

1.4. The Services

Access to a variety of services, such as healthcare, banking, telecommunications, and information centers, must be made available to tourists. Increasing the overall safety and convenience of the destination can be accomplished by developing and maintaining these services. This is of utmost importance for passengers coming from other countries.

2. **The Effects of the Construction of Infrastructure on the Economy**

   2.1. The Generation of Jobs

   The growth of infrastructure results in the creation of job

opportunities in the construction, maintenance, and other associated service sectors. When the infrastructure is fully functional, it will continue to provide employment opportunities in areas such as the hospitality industry, the transportation industry, and the retail sector. The creation of new jobs in the tourism industry can assist in the reduction of unemployment and the stimulation of local economies.

2.2. The Generation of Revenue

An improved tourism infrastructure may result in an increase in the number of visitors as well as longer lengths of stay. This results in increased spending by tourists, which in turn generates significant cash for local businesses, governments, and communities. Consequently, this benefits everyone. This revenue frequently finances the creation of further infrastructure, so establishing a positive feedback cycle.

2.3. Diversification of the Economic System

The economy of a location can benefit from the addition of tourism. Tourism has the potential to bring economic diversification to areas that were previously reliant on a single industry, such as agriculture or manufacturing, and this can be beneficial to those places. This diversity has the potential to make the regional economy more resistant to the effects of shocks from the outside.

2.4. The Attraction of Investments

A location that boasts up-to-date infrastructure that is also well-maintained has a greater chance of luring in investment. Businesses are more likely to invest in regions that have strong transportation links, reliable utilities, and an appealing environment. All of these factors may be improved through the development of infrastructure, which is another reason why these regions are attractive to businesses.

3. Environmentally Responsible and Sustainable Infrastructure

3.1. Responsible Travel and Tourism

The development of sustainable tourist practices can be helped along by infrastructure improvements. It is possible to lessen tourism's negative effects on the environment by investments in environmentally friendly modes of transportation, energy-efficient lodgings, and trash reduction practices. Not only are environmentally friendly tourist activities beneficial, but they also satisfy the ever-increasing demand for socially and environmentally conscious vacations.

3.2. The Protection of Cultural Assets

It is necessary, in order to maintain the character of a place, to develop infrastructure that acknowledges, respects, and celebrates the local culture and tradition. This includes the establishment of visitor centers and facilities for cultural interpretation, as well as the incorporation of classic architectural styles into the building process.

3.3 The Principles of Accessibility and Inclusivity

The building of infrastructure ought to place an emphasis on inclusivity and accessibility. This entails making certain that all guests, regardless of their age, level of physical ability, or cultural heritage, are able to take full advantage of the amenities provided by the location. This includes both facilities and services geared toward people with disabilities as well as information available in several languages.

4. Obstacles and Potential Landmines in the Development of Infrastructure

4.1. Excessive Tourism

The overdevelopment of infrastructure at famous areas can lead to an increase in tourism, which in turn can result in congestion, the degradation of the natural environment, and the loss of cultural traditions. It is vital to find a balance between enticing tourists and maintaining the natural and cultural resources of the area. Both of these goals are essential.

4.2. The Impact on the Environment

The expansion of infrastructure can have substantial effects on the surrounding environment, including the destruction of habitat, the contamination of surrounding areas, and the consumption of available resources. To reduce the severity of these consequences, it is essential to put environmentally responsible and sustainable building methods into place.

4.3. Exorbitant Fees

Creating and maintaining infrastructure may be an expensive endeavor, particularly for less
developed locations that have less available resources. It can be a substantial difficulty to strike a balance between the requirement for contemporary infrastructure and the restrictions of available financial resources.

4.4. Displacement in Social Structure

Infrastructure development, particularly in urban areas, can have the unintended consequence of social displacement. This can occur when local residents are compelled to relocate as a result of increased property values or other effects of development. This can result in socioeconomic inequity as well as a loss of the distinctive personality of a community.

5. Methods of Environmentally Responsible Infrastructure Growth in the Tourism Industry

5.1. Planning With Responsibility

To strike a balance between the need for the expansion of infrastructure and the need to preserve the environment, responsible planning is important. This requires taking into consideration the destination's carrying capacity, putting in place zoning rules, and developing comprehensive plans that put an emphasis on responsible tourism.

5.2. Partnerships Between the Public and Private Sectors

Infrastructure projects can be more easily funded and carried out with the support of collaboration between the public and private sectors. The creation of high-quality infrastructure can be ensured through the use of public-private partnerships, which can maximize the use of resources, knowledge, and capital.

5.3. Environmentally Friendly Technology

It is possible to reduce the negative effects that new infrastructure development has on the surrounding environment by making use of environmentally friendly technologies. These technologies include renewable energy sources, efficient transportation, and green building practices. Additionally, it satisfies the ever-increasing need for eco-friendly vacations.

5.4. Participation in the Community

Participation of local communities in the decision-making process throughout the building of infrastructure assures that the projects will fulfill the requirements and expectations of local citizens. It also has the potential to instill a sense of ownership and a dedication to the continued protection of the destination's identity.

5.5. Administration of Guests

The use of visitor management tactics, such as crowd control measures and visiting quotas for sensitive sites, can help ameliorate some of the problems that can arise as a result of overtourism.

5.6. Repairs and Continual Maintenance

It is imperative that infrastructure be well maintained in order to ensure its continued usefulness and appeal over the long run. To safeguard the value of the investment made in infrastructure, routine maintenance, which may include repairs and restorations, is required.

6. Prospective Developments in the Tourism Industry's Physical Infrastructure

6.1. Infrastructure that is Both Green and Sustainable

The development of infrastructure that is both environmentally friendly and sustainable will continue to receive increased attention. The use of ecologically friendly building methods, alternative forms of energy, and transportation, as well as low-impact modes of transit, will be given top priority.

6.2. Intelligence-Based Technologies

The implementation of intelligent technologies, such as mobile apps that provide information to tourists, contactless check-ins at hotels, and data-driven management, will result in an improved tourist experience and more efficient use of the underlying infrastructure.

6.3. Remote and Isolated Regions of the Country

As worries about overtourism become more prevalent, there will be a movement toward the development of infrastructure in rural and less-visited areas in order to spread tourism more equitably and encourage people to discover sites that are off the beaten path.

6.4. Planning for Resilience

The requirement for resilience planning in the construction of physical infrastructure will be driven by climate change and other environmental concerns. Among these measures is the modification of existing infrastructure so that it can survive the effects of extreme weather and rising sea levels.

6.5 The spirit of inclusion

The movement toward inclusiveness will continue, and there will be an increased emphasis on making infrastructure accessible to all tourists, irrespective of the physical abilities, ages, or cultural backgrounds that they may bring with them.

The expansion of physical infrastructure is an important part of the tourist sector because it lays the groundwork for luring visitors and caring for their needs once they arrive. Nevertheless, the construction of sustainable infrastructure is absolutely necessary in order to guarantee the long-term viability of tourism as well as the location itself. It is essential to pay close attention to the delicate balancing act that must be performed between preservation and development, economic expansion and environmental safeguarding, accessibility and inclusiveness. Destinations have the potential to maintain their growth and success while simultaneously preserving the natural and cultural resources that make them one-of-a-kind through the implementation of infrastructure techniques that are sustainable and responsible.

6.1 Transportation and Accessibility

People, places, and cultures can all be linked to one another through the power of transportation, which is becoming an increasingly important factor in our increasingly interconnected world. It is essential to modern living and makes possible a wide range of activities, from routine commuting to international travel. The significance of transportation goes much beyond that of sheer convenience; it also holds the key to accessibility, allowing citizens to access education, work, healthcare, and leisure opportunities. In the course of this in-depth investigation, we dig into the relevance of mobility and accessibility, the issues encountered by many communities, as well as the tactics and technologies that are paving the way for a more inclusive and connected world.

1. **The Importance of Different Modes of Transport**

    1.1. The Expansion of the Economy

    The expansion of the economy can be attributed to improvements in transportation. Businesses, commerce, and the development of new jobs can all benefit from efficient transportation systems because they facilitate the rapid and cost-effective movement of both goods and people. This, in turn, propels the growth of the economy and leads to wealth.

    1.2. The Ability to Connect

    Communities and regions can be connected through the use of transportation, which opens up access to vital services and resources. It helps persons in rural areas have access to healthcare, educational possibilities, and career prospects in metropolitan areas, bridging the gap between the two.

    1.3 The Process of Globalization

    Transportation paves the way for globalization to become a reality. Through the promotion of global commerce, the sharing of cultural experiences, and the expansion of tourism opportunities, it connects the world in ways that were previously inconceivable.

1.4. Interaction with Other People

People's ability to travel to see family and friends, go to events, and discover new locations is one way that transportation facilitates more social engagement. This sense of connectedness and movement is essential to keeping social bonds alive and keeping one's health in good standing.

2. Obstacles in the Fields of Transportation and Accessibility

2.1. Deficits in the Infrastructure

Accessibility faces a substantial obstacle due to deficiencies in infrastructure, which are particularly prevalent in developing regions. The lack of adequate public transportation systems, inadequate road networks, and restricted air and maritime connectivity can be detrimental to economic development and quality of life.

2.2. Differences in Socioeconomic Status

The availability of transportation can often be unequally distributed, which can result in socioeconomic inequality. Residents of low-income communities may not have access to dependable transportation choices, which makes it more difficult for them to access important services, educational opportunities, and employment prospects.

2.3. Negative Effects on the Environment

Many forms of transportation, including automobiles and airplanes, are responsible for contributing to the deterioration of the environment as a result of the emissions of greenhouse gases and other pollutants. It is a huge problem to strike a balance between the requirements of accessibility and those of environmental sustainability.

2.4. Availability to All

It is a difficult challenge to ensure that all people, regardless of their physical limitations or any other element, have access to and are included in all aspects of the transportation system. A significant number of public transportation systems and other types of infrastructure are not designed to be accessible to people who have impairments.

3. **Methods for Enhancing Transportation and Increasing Accessibility**

   3.1. Investments in Physical Infrastructure

   Increasing one's accessibility can be accomplished in large part by investing in various forms of transportation infrastructure. It should be a top priority for governments and organizations to construct and maintain networks of roads, railroads, and airports as well as public transit systems.

   3.2. Partnerships Between the Public and Private Sectors

   The improvement of transportation networks can benefit from public-private partnerships, which can make the most of available resources and expertise. The development of infrastructure can be funded by private corporations, while the operation of transportation services can be regulated and monitored by government agencies.

   3.3. Transportation That Is Sustainable

   The negative effects that transportation has on the environment can be mitigated by encouraging more sustainable modes of transportation, such as public transit, cycling, walking, and electric vehicles. This will also make transportation more accessible.

   3.4. Sense of Inclusion

   It is vital to design both the infrastructure of transportation and the cars themselves such that they are accessible to everyone. This includes making available accessible modes of transportation for people of all ages, including those with physical limitations, senior citizens, and families with young children.

   3.5. Developments and Advancements in Technology

   Transportation and accessibility are undergoing fundamental shifts as a result of developments in technology. People's access to various modes of transportation is being revolutionized by developments such as ride-sharing services, electric scooters, and driverless vehicles.

4. **Developments in Methods of Transportation and Ease of Access**

   4.1. Self-Driving Cars and Trucks

   The introduction of autonomous vehicles, commonly referred to as self-driving automobiles, has the potential to bring about a sea change in the transportation sector. They have the potential to improve mobility for people with impairments, hence reducing the number of accidents that occur and making roadways safer.

   4.2. Rail Travel at a High Speed

   High-speed rail networks, which may be found in nations such as Japan and France, provide a means of transportation that is both effective and kind to the environment. These networks have the potential to link cities, cut down on travel times, and stimulate economic expansion.

   4.3. The Hyperloop

   The hyperloop is a high-speed transportation system that employs low-pressure tubes to propel pods at tremendous speeds. Elon Musk is the brains behind the concept of the hyperloop, which he invented. If it were to become a reality, it would completely transform long-distance travel by making it both speedier and more environmentally friendly.

   4.4. Mobility as a Service (also known as MaaS) and Ride-Sharing

   Convenience and accessibility are two benefits that can be gained from using ride-sharing services such as Uber and Lyft in conjunction with Mobility as a Service (MaaS) platforms. These services offer several possibilities for on-demand transportation at prices that are frequently lower than those of typical taxis.

   4.5. Mobility via Electric Vehicles

   Both electric cars (EVs) and electric scooters are gaining ground as viable modes of mobility in metropolitan areas. Electric vehicles cut down on pollutants and lessen our reliance on fossil fuels, while electric scooters offer a practical and environmentally responsible method to travel shorter distances.

5. **The Prospects for Transportation and Accessibility in the Future**

5.1. Transportation That Is Both Eco-Friendly And Sustainable

The continued emphasis on sustainable practices will be the primary impetus behind the creation of ecologically responsible modes of transportation. The adoption of electric vehicles, renewable energy sources, and creative approaches to urban design will all help to make the future more sustainable.

5.2. Mobility That Is Shared

The sharing economy, which is distinguished by shared mobility services such as ride-sharing and bike-sharing, will continue to experience significant expansion. This movement encourages easily accessible and reasonably priced modes of transportation options.

5.3. Mobility as a Service (also known as MaaS)

It is expected that MaaS systems, which integrate numerous transportation services into a single platform that is user-friendly and accessible, would become increasingly common. These platforms provide a "one-stop shop" for various transportation-related services in an effort to make individual travel more convenient.

5.4 The state of being hyperconnected

Hyperconnectivity will become possible as a result of developments in technology and data-driven solutions, which will make it possible for transportation systems to become more effective and user-friendly. There will be major contributions from artificial intelligence, the Internet of Things (IoT), and activities pertaining to smart cities to the improvement of mobility and accessibility.

5.5. Design That Is Inclusive

The movement toward inclusive design will eventually result in transportation systems that are able to meet the needs of all users, irrespective of their age, level of physical ability, or cultural heritage. The development of a transportation system that is accessible to all people will receive a greater amount of priority.

Transportation is the lifeblood of accessibility, connecting people to necessary services, employment, educational opportunities, and recreational opportunities. It is the lifeblood of accessible. It is a driving force for economic growth and globalization, but it also offers issues linked to infrastructure gaps, social inequality, environmental damage, and inclusivity. Despite its importance, these challenges are not insurmountable. Strategies such as investing in infrastructure, public-private partnerships, environmentally friendly transit options, inclusion, and technological advancements are essential if we are to find solutions to these difficulties.

Sustainability, shared mobility, platforms that offer Mobility as a Service, hyperconnectivity, and inclusive design will be the defining characteristics of the accessibility and transportation landscape of the future. People's access to transportation will continue to be transformed as a result of developments in technology, data-driven solutions, and innovative urban design. As a result, access to transportation will become more effective, user-friendly, and inclusive. The purpose of this endeavor is to bring about a future in which transportation not only links individuals and locations but also assures that all people, regardless of their origins or levels of capability, are able to take use of the advantages of accessibility.

6.2 Accommodations and Tourism

The provision of lodgings as locations not only for securing one's rest and recharging one's batteries but also as essential elements of the experience enjoyed by tourists is essential to the success of the tourism sector. Accommodations occur in a broad variety of forms, ranging from opulent hotels and quaint bed-and-breakfast inns to secluded wilderness lodges and lively hostels. Each of these types offers a distinctive slice of the culture and hospitality of the location that it calls home. In the course of this in-depth investigation, we look into the significance of lodgings in the tourism industry, the various types of accommodations that are available, and the factors that influence the decisions that tourists make. Additionally, we explore the role that accommodations play in the enhancement of the overarching travel experience, as well as economic growth and the maintenance of a sustainable tourism industry.

1. **The Importance of Lodging Facilities to the Tourism Industry**
   1.1. A Place of Safety and Solace
   Travelers need a place to stay while they are exploring a destination so that they may feel safe and comfortable. Accommodations provide both of these needs. The standard and personality of one's lodgings can have a big impact on the journey as a whole; this is true whether one is staying in a quaint cottage in the woods or a stylish hotel in the metropolis.
   1.2. The Immersion Travel Experience
   There are many varying degrees of cultural and environmental immersion that can be had depending on the sort of lodging chosen at a vacation spot. It is possible for travelers to have a more genuine experience by booking a stay at a local establishment, such as a riad in Morocco or a log cabin in the Canadian Rockies.
   1.3. The Happiness of the Passengers
   Traveler happiness is directly correlated to the quality of their accommodations. A vacation that is memorable and one that is disappointing can be turned around thanks to a pleasant and well-maintained place to stay, which can result in return business and favorable word-of-mouth recommendations.
   1.4. The Contribution to the Economy
   The hospitality industry is one of the most important contributors to the economy of a place. It not only helps local businesses like farming, artisanal goods production, and the culinary arts, but it also brings in cash through dining, spa services, and lodging rates.

2. Different Categories of Lodging

2.1. Accommodations

Hotels are one of the most common types of accommodations available and can range from being inexpensive to being on par with the most opulent resorts in terms of amenities and ambiance. They range in size, amenities, and level of service to accommodate a wide variety of traveler requirements.

2.2. Vacation Spots

Resorts are a type of destination lodging that typically contain a wide range of amenities for guests, including a selection of dining options, swimming pools, spas, and other recreational facilities. They are intended to provide guests with an all-encompassing vacation experience.

2.3. Bed and Breakfasts, often known as B&Bs

Inns and bed and breakfasts provide guests a more private and individualized hotel experience. They normally have a small number of available rooms, but they are well-known for serving breakfasts made from scratch and for interacting with customers on a more personable level.

2.4. Guesthouses

Hostels are low-cost lodging options that cater to younger tourists who are more open to experiencing new things. They provide accommodations in the style of a shared dormitory, which makes them an economical option for budget travelers.

2.5. Holiday Homes and Apartments

Cabins, apartments, cottages, and villas are some of the types of real estate that can be rented
out by vacationers for stays of a shorter duration and fall under the category of "vacation rentals." They offer additional space as well as more freedom for guests.

2.6. Accommodations That Are Both Boutique and Unique

Travelers who are looking for an unusual or out-of-the-way experience will find that boutique hotels, treehouses, yurts, and other types of unusual lodgings offer experiences that are one of a kind.

3. **Considerations That Go Into Making Accommodation Selections**

    3.1. Financial Plan

    When selecting a place to stay, one's financial situation is a crucial consideration. There are a variety of lodging alternatives available to tourists, ranging from low-cost hostels to high-end luxury hotels, and vacationers choose those that are most appropriate for their budgets.

    3.2. Position in Space

    Important factors to take into account are proximity to natural landscapes, urban hubs, and tourist sites. Most of the time, vacationers look for lodging options that are situated in convenient areas so that they can get the most out of their trip.

    3.3. The Conveniences

    The decision-making process is heavily influenced by the availability of various amenities. It's possible that guests will place a higher value on amenities like swimming pools, Wi-Fi, restaurants, and fitness centers.

    3.4. Specific Preferences of the Individual

    The personal preferences of travelers, such as the yearning for a romantic ambiance, a family-friendly environment, or a policy that allows them to bring their pets, have a considerable impact on the decisions they make.

    3.5 Ratings and Comments on Reviews and Recommendations

    It is possible for online evaluations, suggestions from friends and family, and comments from prior guests to have a significant impact on the accommodations that a visitor chooses to book.

4. **The Role of Lodging Establishments in the Tourism Industry**

    4.1. The Growth of the Economy

    The expansion of an area's economy can be directly attributed to its variety of lodging options. They create a significant amount of cash through accommodation bookings, eating, and additional services, which in turn leads to the development of jobs and increased investment in local businesses.

4.2. Marketing of Tourist Attractions

The marketing of a destination relies heavily on the accommodations that are offered there. Iconic hotels and resorts frequently become emblems of a location because they attract tourists and showcase the local culture as well as the natural beauty of the region.

4.3. Participation in a Culture

Some places to stay provide guests with one-of-a-kind opportunities for cultural immersion. Travelers who choose to lodge in traditional or historic establishments have the opportunity to engage with the local customs, traditions, and legacy.

4.4. Long-Term Viability

Accommodations that stress eco-friendly methods and responsible tourism are referred to as sustainable. They limit their influence on the environment by preserving natural resources, cutting down on waste, and giving back to the communities in which they operate.

5. Obstacles and Long-Term Viability in the Accommodations Industry

5.1. Excessive Tourism

Overtourism can result in an increase in the number of people visiting popular areas, which can have a negative effect on both the quality of the tourist experience and the environment. It is of the utmost importance to manage accommodation capacity and to promote locations that are off the usual path.

5.2. Repercussions on the Environment

Because of their high levels of energy and water consumption as well as trash production, many types of lodging leave a significant mark on the environment. It is vital to implement sustainable measures in order to lessen the impact of this, such as designing for energy efficiency and reducing waste.

5.3. Preservation of Cultural Assets

It is possible for a destination's traditions and sense of authenticity to deteriorate over time if the accommodations there are insensitive to the local culture and heritage. It is essential to strike a balance between the preservation of cultural traditions and the expansion of lodging options.

5.4. Differences in Economic Conditions

When local communities do not benefit proportionally from economic progress, it can lead to income inequities, despite the fact that accommodations contribute to economic growth.

In order to find a solution to this problem, you will need to develop strategies that encourage community involvement and revenue sharing.

6. Methods of Environmentally Responsible Lodging

6.1. Design That Is Kind to the Environment

The design and construction procedures of lodging establishments should be environmentally friendly. These practices should include energy-efficient architecture, renewable energy sources, and green building materials.

6.2. Manage Responsibly All Available Resources

In order to lessen their impact on the environment, lodging facilities should practice responsible resource management and adhere to best practices in water and waste reduction, as well as energy and resource conservation.

6.3. Participation in the Community

Engaging with the communities that surround an accommodation can help that establishment become more responsible and make a positive contribution to the destination. This can entail supporting local businesses, employing local staff, and working together with local craftspeople.

6.4. Food Prepared Using Environmentally

The environmental effect of food services can be decreased by supporting local agriculture and offering cuisine that is seasonal, made with locally sourced ingredients, and sustainable.

6.5. Awareness and Educational Initiatives

It is vital to educate passengers about responsible tourism practices, such as decreasing trash and saving water, in order to promote sustainable travel.

7. The Prospects for Lodging within the Tourism Industry

7.1. Long-Term Viability

Travelers will continue to look for lodging options that are in line with the environmentally concerned ideals they hold, thus the emphasis on sustainability will only increase. This includes the reduction of trash and energy consumption, as well as support for the communities in which we live.

7.2. Technology

The use of technology will become an increasingly important component of the whole stay at a hotel. Convenience and individualization will both be improved because to developments such as smartphone check-in, intelligent room controls, and virtual concierges.

7.3. Wellness and overall sense of well-being

The health and happiness of guests will soon be the primary concern of lodging establishments. The availability of lodging will include a variety of features that promote health and wellness, such as exercise centers, spaces dedicated to mindfulness, and healthy dining alternatives.

7.4. Experiences That Are Both Authentic And Cultural

Accommodations that provide cultural immersion and authentic experiences will become increasingly desirable among tourists. The ability to stay in accommodations that are representative of the local culture and heritage will be a major selling point.

7.5. The ability to personalize

Accommodations will make every effort to give personalized experiences by customizing their services to meet the interests and requirements of individual tourists.

Travelers are provided with shelter, comfort, and a feeling of location by their accommodations, making them an essential component of the tourism experience. They make a contribution to the tourism industry's continued economic growth, marketing of destinations, cultural immersion, and environmental sustainability. Sustainable practices are beginning to emerge as a solution to the problems that are caused by overtourism, the influence that tourism has on the environment, the preservation of cultural traditions, and economic imbalances. In the future of the tourism industry, accommodations will be characterized by sustainability, the integration of technology, wellness and well-being, cultural authenticity, and personalization. This will provide tourists with a wide variety of options to choose from in order to make their trips memorable and contribute to the expansion and continued viability of the tourism industry.

6.3 Public Services and Tourism

The provision of essential public services is an essential component of sustaining and advancing the tourism business. This is important because it helps to ensure that tourists have positive travel experiences that run smoothly. These services include a variety of important facilities and amenities that are supplied by the government or the public sector. They contribute to the general health and happiness of tourists by improving their experience. Not only does the incorporation of effective public services assist in the operation of tourist activities in a seamless manner, but it also makes a contribution to the growth and long-term viability of the tourism industry as a whole.

Infrastructure and Facilities: The important facilities and infrastructure in a society, such as roads, airports, and public transit systems, are the responsibility of the public services and must be maintained and expanded upon. The ease with which tourists may access and navigate places is a crucial component that contributes to the overall quality of their vacation experience.

Safety and Security: The establishment and upkeep of law enforcement, emergency response teams, and health services are examples of the public services that contribute to the safety and security of vacationers. It is essential to provide a safe and protected setting in order to cultivate a sense of trust and comfort among passengers, which in turn encourages them to venture out and become involved in the destination.

Information and Direction: Public services include information centers, tourist information desks, and guides that offer useful insights into the cultural history of the area, as well as safety advice. These centers and desks can be found in most tourist destinations. Information that is easily accessible to tourists improves their comprehension of the destination, which in turn enables them to make decisions based on accurate information and fosters a greater appreciation of the local culture and environment.

Management of the Environment: The management of garbage, conservation efforts, and the protection of natural resources are all examples of environmental management activities that are frequently supervised by public agencies. The use of environmentally friendly business methods and the protection of natural landscapes both contribute to the long-term profitability of tourist destinations. This ensures that these places will continue to be appealing to tourists in the years to come.

Not only can governments increase the amount of tourists they receive by effectively delivering these services, but they can also ensure that their cultural and natural riches will continue to be preserved for future generations. The provision of public services acts as an essential pillar of support, making possible the expansion and development of the tourism industry while simultaneously creating a favorable and enlightening experience for tourists.

6.4 Infrastructure Investments and Returns

Investments in infrastructure are essential for the expansion and development of nations, as they help to foster economic growth and contribute to an overall improvement in the quality of life. These investments include things like a country's transportation networks, energy systems, communication technology, and public facilities, and they serve as the fundamental basis for how a country operates. The returns on investments in infrastructure are enormous due to the multiple economic, social, and environmental benefits that are brought about by these investments.

Economic Growth Investments in infrastructure not only create jobs but also increase overall productivity, which in turn stimulates economic growth. A substantial number of people are employed on construction projects, as well as in the operation and maintenance of infrastructure facilities, which results in the creation of jobs. In addition, effective energy networks and transportation systems cut down on production costs, boost trade, and entice investments, all of which contribute to the growth of the national economy.

Productivity Boost: A well-developed infrastructure makes it possible for various industries to achieve better levels of productivity. For example, time and money can be saved thanks to the efficiency of today's transportation and communication networks, which allow for the rapid flow of both commodities and information. This, in turn, boosts the competitiveness of enterprises, which encourages innovation and contributes to the expansion of the economy.

Enhanced Connectivity Thanks to improvements in infrastructure, areas have better connectivity, which makes them more accessible to businesses as well as tourists. Digital infrastructure, such as high-speed internet, connects individuals and businesses to global markets. Physical infrastructure, such as highways, airports, and ports, make it easier for people and commodities to move throughout the country and the world.

The quality of life of the citizens is also strongly impacted by the expenditures made in infrastructure. The availability of dependable public services, such as clean water and sanitation, as well as medical facilities, all contribute to an improvement in overall health and well-being. Congestion in the roads and pollution in the air are alleviated thanks to public transportation networks, which also improve living conditions in cities. Moreover, financial investments made in educational and cultural institutions help to the growth and enrichment of both the individual and the culture.

Sustainability in Relation to the Environment: Investments in environmentally responsible infrastructure encourage the reduction of waste and improvement of resource utilization. Investments in renewable energy sources, such as wind and solar power, for instance, bring about reductions in emissions of greenhouse gases and a lessening of dependency on fossil fuels. In addition, sustainable urban planning and green building methods can lead to decreased energy consumption and the production of garbage, which is beneficial to both the environment and the economy.

Providing critical services to communities that are not already receiving them is one way in which infrastructure investments might help address socioeconomic disparities.

In the name of social justice, initiatives such as rural electrification, access to clean water, and inexpensive housing improve the living conditions of underserved communities as well as the opportunities available to such populations.

Infrastructure investments in disaster-resilient facilities, such as flood control systems and earthquake-resistant structures, can save lives and lessen the economic effect of natural catastrophes. Resilience and disaster preparedness are synonymous terms. It is essential for both disaster management and recovery to make investments in infrastructure that can both withstand such occurrences and recover after they have occurred.

Chapter 7

Marketing and Promotion

Marketing and public relations are essential parts of today's successful business strategies. They comprise a wide variety of strategies and technologies with the goals of recruiting new consumers, keeping existing ones engaged, and keeping existing ones loyal. In an era that is characterized by swift technology breakthroughs and evolving consumer habits, marketing and promotion have altered and adapted to new paradigms in order to remain relevant. This in-depth investigation will delve into the world of marketing and promotion, covering the strategies, trends, and impacts of these essential components in today's ever-changing business scene.

1. **A Comprehension of Advertising and Public Relations**
   1.1. **A Definitive Exposition of Marketing**
   The process of developing, conveying, providing, and trading offerings that are of benefit to consumers, business clients, business partners, and society as a whole is referred to as marketing. It encompasses a wide variety of actions, from researching the market and developing new products to advertising and making

sales; all of these operations are geared at satisfying the requirements and preferences of the client.

1.2. Promotion in the context of marketing

Along with product, price, and location (sometimes known as distribution), promotion is one of the four Ps that make up marketing. It includes all of the communication and message tactics that are employed to educate customers, sway their opinions, and shape the way they behave. Advertising, public relations, sales promotions, and a variety of other forms of content creation are all examples of promotional methods.

2. **Tactics for Advertising and Public Relations**

   2.1. The Division of the Market

The process of splitting a large potential customer base into a number of smaller, more manageable subgroups that share certain criteria is known as market segmentation. This tactic gives companies the ability to target particular subsets of customers with their advertising and marketing initiatives, which in turn boosts the efficiency of those companies' campaigns.

2.2. The Marketing of Content

Material marketing is centered on the process of producing and disseminating material that is valuable, pertinent, and consistent with the goal of attracting and engaging a certain audience. Blog entries, films, infographics, and status updates on social media are all examples of the diverse formats that content can take.

2.3. Marketing Through Social Media

Engaging with new and existing consumers is one of the primary goals of social media marketing, which makes use of widely used social networking platforms like Facebook, Instagram, Twitter, and LinkedIn. It incorporates organic (non-paid) as well as paid marketing methods.

2.4 Marketing Based on Influence

Collaborating with individuals who have a sizeable and enthusiastic following in a certain field is an essential part of the influencer marketing strategy. These influencers advocate a brand's products or services to their audience, which frequently results in increased visibility and reputation for the brand in question.

2.5. Search Engine Optimization (SEO)

SEO, or search engine optimization, is the process of improving a website's exposure in search engine results by optimizing the content and structure of the website. Implementing efficient SEO methods helps firms rank higher in the pages of search engine results, which in turn leads to an increase in organic traffic.

2.6. Email Marketing

Email marketing is still an effective method for targeting a certain demographic of consumers. Email is a tool that marketers use to send updates, promotions, and personalized information directly to the inboxes of their subscribers.

2.7. Relations with the Public

Building and preserving a positive image for a company or organization is the primary objective of public relations, also known as PR. PR experts are responsible for cultivating good connections with the media, managing crises, and promoting the success stories and achievements of their clients' brands.

2.8. Advertisements That Are Paid For

Paid advertising encompasses a wide variety of advertising formats, both online and offline, including pay-per-click (PPC) advertising, display ads, advertising on social media platforms, and commercials broadcast on traditional media platforms like television and radio.

3. Current Trends in Marketing and Promotion

3.1. Customization of Contents

Consumers are becoming more accustomed to anticipating individualized experiences. Automated marketing, data analytics, and artificial intelligence (AI) are paving the way for more personalized content and product recommendations to be developed.

3.2. Marketing with Videos

The consumption of video content across websites and social media platforms is currently at an all-time high. This trend includes a variety of elements, including live streaming, video advertisements, and user-generated material.

3.3. Optimization for Voice Searches

The proliferation of voice-activated devices such as Google Home and Amazon's Alexa has resulted in the modification of material to better accommodate voice search queries. This trend is changing how brands approach search engine optimization (SEO) and content production.

3.4. Content Generated by the User

Content that was generated by users, like as reviews, testimonials, and postings made on social media, has a significant impact on the purchasing decisions that potential customers make. User-generated content is becoming an increasingly important component of marketing methods employed by companies.

3.5. Social Business as an Industry

The e-commerce capabilities of social media platforms are rapidly developing, and users will soon be able to shop straight within social network apps. The barrier between social connection and online commerce is becoming increasingly blurry as a result of this development.

3.6. Ethical and Environmentally Responsible Marketing

The interest of consumers in purchasing goods from companies that demonstrate social and environmental responsibility is growing. Efforts in marketing that put an emphasis on ethical and environmentally responsible business operations are gaining traction.

4. The Influence of Advertising and Public Relations

4.1. Awareness of the Brand

Brand awareness may be increased through the use of effective marketing and promotion techniques, which in turn makes a brand more recognized to customers and easier for them to recall.

4.2. Engagement of the Customer

Marketing efforts that are engaging are good for building relationships between brands and customers, which in turn encourages customer loyalty and repeat business.

4.3. Sales and Financial Results

At the end of the day, the purpose of marketing and promotion initiatives is to boost sales and bring in income for businesses. A campaign that is carried out effectively has the potential to have a major impact on the financial success of a firm.

4.4. Development of the Market

A company's market reach can be expanded geographically and demographically through marketing and promotion, which in turn can open up new chances for the company's growth.

4.5. The Creation of the Product

Product creation is frequently informed by consumer feedback and market research collected through marketing initiatives. This enables organizations to better tailor their services to the requirements and preferences of their target audiences.

4.6. Advantage in the Competitive Market

A competitive advantage can be gained by the implementation of successful marketing tactics, which distinguish a brand from its competitors in the eyes of customers.

5. Considerations Regarding Ethical Behavior in Marketing and Promotion

5.1. Data Privacy and Security

The General Data Protection Regulation (GDPR) and the California Consumer Privacy Act (CCPA) are two examples of severe privacy requirements that must be adhered to in the process of collecting and using data on individual consumers.

5.2. Be Honest in Your Advertising

Advertisements that are deceptive or misleading should never be used. This includes providing accurate descriptions of products, providing reviews in an honest manner, and providing clear disclaimers in any sponsored content.

5.3. Our Obligation to the Community

It is becoming more common for consumers to anticipate that businesses will take into account the social and environmental impact of their operations and engage in responsible business practices. Consumers frequently show their support for businesses that share their morals and beliefs.

5.4. Inclusiveness as well as Diversity

In terms of marketing and promotion, diversity and inclusiveness are quite important. Not only is it ethical to represent a wide range of demographics and points of view, but it also has a greater chance of resonating with a wider variety of customers.

Marketing and promotion are vital components of every business strategy that is intended to be successful. They comprise a wide variety of approaches and instruments, and they are continuously undergoing development in response to shifting patterns of consumer behavior and the development of new technologies. Brands can increase their visibility, engage their target audience, and ultimately drive development and success in a market where there is a lot of competition if they have a good understanding of effective marketing and promotion techniques and put those strategies into practice. However, in order to ensure that these efforts have a positive and long-lasting influence on customers as well as society in general, they must be led by ethical considerations such as the protection of personal data, transparency, and social responsibility.

7.1 The Role of Marketing in Attracting Tourists

In a lot of different places all around the world, tourism is an important engine of both economic growth and cultural interaction. Attracting tourists and assuring the success of businesses and locations that are dependent on tourism are both directly tied to the marketing efforts that are put out. When operating in a business that is notoriously cut-throat, having effective marketing methods might be the difference between a tourist site that is thriving and one that is having trouble drawing in customers. This in-depth investigation digs into the essential role that marketing plays in luring tourists, covering the tactics, techniques, and impact that marketing activities have in the tourism industry. Specifically, this investigation focuses on the function that marketing plays in attracting tourists.

1. **The Importance of Marketing for the Tourism Industry**
   1.1. Our Financial Role in the Community
   Revenue is generated through lodging, transportation, dining, and entertainment establishments, as well as a variety of activities that are directly or indirectly tied to tourism, making tourism a significant contributor to many nations' economies. A successful marketing campaign will attract tourists, which will in turn drive economic growth and the creation of jobs.
   1.2. Intercultural Communication
   People of varying origins and locations are brought together through the medium of tourism, which in turn helps to encourage cultural exchange. The marketing of a destination helps promote the one-of-a-kind cultural experiences and attractions that it has to offer, which in turn encourages tourists to travel to new places and become more knowledgeable about other cultures.
   1.3. Sustainability with Respect to the Environment
   The promotion of tourist practices that are responsible and sustainable can benefit from marketing efforts. Destinations can ensure that they will continue to be appealing and profitable in the long run by promoting eco-friendly tourism and the preservation of natural resources.
   1.4. A Diversified Offering
   The promotion of many facets of a location, such as historical landmarks and natural wonders as well as festivals and gastronomic experiences, can contribute to the diversification of the economy if tourism marketing is done correctly. The economy

will be less reliant on a single sector as a result of this diversification.

2. **Marketing Strategies for the Tourism Industry**

   2.1. Branding of the Destination

   In order to successfully attract tourists, it is vital to have a strong and distinct brand for the place. An effective branding strategy conveys a destination's character, culture, and experiences to potential visitors, which helps the destination stand out in a crowded market.

   2.2. Marketing in the Digital Age

   Promotion of tourist destinations is currently being led by digital marketing. It encompasses methods such as email marketing, social media marketing, search engine optimization (SEO), content marketing, and online advertising campaigns. These methods enable locations to more effectively communicate with audiences all across the world.

   2.3. Marketing Based on Influence

   When you work together with travel bloggers and other influencers, you can create material that is genuine, interesting, and likely to resonate with future travelers. It is possible for influencers to pique their followers' interest in a destination by highlighting its unique experiences, cultural offerings, and attractions.

   2.4. The Generation of Content

   It is crucial to have material that is high-quality and interesting in order to attract and keep

   tourists. Examples of such content include videos, blog articles, and social media updates. Content that is not only informative but also visually beautiful both delivers useful information to travelers and stimulates them to explore a destination.

   2.5. Relationships of Partnership and Cooperation

   Working together with airlines, tour operators, and travel agents can help a destination become more accessible to a wider audience. A destination's accessibility and attraction to tourists can be improved through collaborative marketing efforts and the creation of attractive package deals.

3. **Methods for Advertising Tourism**

   3.1. Websites That Serve as Destinations

   Many times, the initial point of contact with a potential visitor is through the destination website, which should be both well-designed and helpful. Websites should provide valuable material, easy navigation, and booking choices for a variety of activities and lodgings.

   3.2. Sites and Services for Social Media

   The use of social media platforms such as Instagram, Facebook, and Twitter enables travel locations to interact with a large audience and display their attractions by means of still photographs, motion pictures, and real-time updates.

   3.3. Online Travel Agencies (often abbreviated as OTAs)

   Travel locations can contact passengers wishing to book lodgings, flights, and excursions online by partnering with online travel firms like Expedia and Booking.com, which provide a platform for such transactions.

   3.4. Centers for Visitor and Tourist Information

   Visitors can receive individualized advice at tourist information centers, which might include support in trip planning as well as the provision of brochures and maps. When it comes to attracting tourists to a particular location, these centers are essential touchpoints.

   3.5. Printed Materials for Marketing

   Traditional marketing techniques such as brochures, flyers, and other promotional materials are still utilized to deliver information to travelers about a destination and the attractions that it offers.

4. **The Effects That Tourism Advertising Has**

   4.1. An Increase in the Amount of Tourist Traffic

   An rise in the number of tourists who visit a location as a direct result of successful marketing activities is one of the primary drivers of economic expansion in that location. These efforts also assist in the redistribution of tourists to sites that are less congested or off the beaten path.

4.2. The Growth of the Economy

The location sees an increase in economic growth as a direct result of increased tourist traffic. Because tourists spend money on things like lodging, meals, shopping, and a variety of activities, they help local companies and contribute to the development of jobs.

4.3. The Image of the Destination and Its Reputation

Marketing has a significant impact on the image and reputation of a destination. A destination's reputation can be improved through strategic branding and marketing campaigns that are successful, which in turn can attract repeat visitors and word-of-mouth recommendations.

4.4. The Protection of Cultural Assets

Marketing initiatives can help raise awareness about how important it is to preserve cultural traditions and to engage in tourism practices that are responsible. Educated tourists have a greater likelihood of respecting cultural heritage sites and making contributions to their maintenance.

4.5. The Long-Term Viability of the Environment

Marketing that promotes sustainable tourism inspires tourists to participate in eco-friendly activities and to patronize locations that place a premium on the preservation of the natural environment. This emphasis on sustainable practices helps to preserve natural resources and preserves the allure of a resort.

5. Obstacles Facing the Marketing of Tourism

5.1. Excessive Tourism

Overtourism can put a strain on resources, contribute to environmental degradation, and have a detrimental influence on the communities that are located there. In order for marketing to be effective, there needs to be a balance struck between promotion and initiatives to address and alleviate overtourism.

5.2. Differences in Economic Conditions

The economic benefits of tourism do not always trickle down to the local communities in the same way in all instances. It is imperative that economic inequalities be addressed, and that local companies and communities be involved in marketing initiatives for tourists.

5.3. Negative Effects on the Environment

It is possible for tourism to have an effect on the environment, in particular when it comes to the consumption of resources and transportation. Marketing should encourage environmentally sustainable behaviors and responsible vacationing.

5.4 Honesty and sincerity

It might be difficult for a location to keep its genuine character in the face of growing numbers of visitors from mass tourism. When marketing a location, the emphasis should be placed on highlighting the distinctive natural and cultural features of the location, while staying away from overly marketed and fake experiences.

6. Ethical Considerations in Tourism Advertising and Promotion

6.1. Integrity and Openness of Communication

When it comes to marketing, honesty and openness are of the utmost importance. All of the pertinent information, including costs and hazards, should be given in a way that is understandable and accurate representations of a place and its services should be included in tourism marketing materials.

6.2. Sensitivity to Other Cultures

The marketing of tourism should show respect and sensitivity to all cultures. It is important to steer clear of any actions that could be considered offensive to local customs and traditions, such as stereotypical behavior, cultural appropriation, and so on.

6.3. A Tourism That Is Responsible

Marketing activities should be directed at promoting tourism that is responsible. It is important that tourists be encouraged to participate in environmentally responsible activities, give their patronage to locally owned enterprises, and show respect for both local traditions and the environment.

6.4. Data Privacy and Security

The protection of one's data privacy is an important aspect of any type of marketing. Personal

information provided by travelers should be handled in a manner that is compliant with any applicable data protection requirements.

The marketing of locations all over the world is an essential component in the process of luring visitors there. For the sake of generating economic growth, encouraging cultural interaction, and preserving the tourism industry's long-term viability, having effective marketing tactics is crucial. Destinations have the ability to attract the attention of passengers, provide them with experiences that they will remember, and help to the growth of their economies by making use of a variety of marketing methods and strategies. When it comes to fostering environmentally responsible and authentic tourism experiences, the importance of ethical issues such as transparency, cultural sensitivity, and responsible tourism practices cannot be overstated. Tourism marketing continues to be a dynamic and influential force, even in a global landscape that is undergoing rapid transformation. This force shapes the future of destinations as well as the experiences they provide for travelers.

7.2 Online and Offline Marketing Strategies

The success of a corporation is directly correlated to its marketing techniques. To be successful in the ever-shifting environment of marketing, companies need to find a middle ground between online and offline methods of communication to effectively engage the consumers they are trying to reach. This all-encompassing investigation will delve into the realm of offline and online marketing techniques, exploring their significance, distinctions, and the various ways in which they can be combined for the best possible results.

1. **Marketing Strategies Utilizing the Internet**
   1.1. Advertising in the Digital Age
   Pay-per-click (PPC) advertising, display adverts, and advertising on social media platforms are all examples of the types of paid online methods that fall under the umbrella of digital advertising. With the help of these strategies, businesses are able to advertise their goods and services to a significant number of internet users.
   1.2. The Marketing of Content
   material marketing is centered on the process of producing and disseminating material that is valuable, pertinent, and consistent with the goal of attracting and engaging a certain audience. Blog entries, films, infographics, and status updates on social media are all examples of the diverse formats that content can take.
   1.3. Marketing Through Social Media
   Engaging with new and existing consumers is one of the primary goals of social media marketing, which makes use of widely used social networking platforms like Facebook, Instagram, Twitter, and LinkedIn. It incorporates organic (non-paid) as well as paid marketing methods.
   1.4. Email Marketing
   Email marketing entails sending email campaigns that are specifically tailored to a list of subscribers. The objective of this tactic is to send personalized material, promotions, and updates to the inboxes of the receivers directly.
   1.5. Search Engine Optimization (SEO)
   SEO, or search engine optimization, is the process of improving a website's exposure in search engine results by optimizing the content and structure of the website. Implementing efficient SEO methods helps firms rank higher in the pages of search engine results, which in turn leads to an increase in organic traffic.

1.6. Marketing Through Influencers

Collaborating with individuals who have a sizeable and enthusiastic following in a certain field is an essential part of the influencer marketing strategy. These influencers advocate a brand's products or services to their audience, which frequently results in increased visibility and reputation for the brand in question.

2. Strategies for Conducting Business Offline

2.1. Advertisements in Print

The term "print advertising" refers to the more conventional types of advertising, such as advertisements published in newspapers and magazines, as well as brochures, flyers, and direct mail. These strategies are effective for addressing local audiences as well as target demographics in a certain area.

2.2. Advertisements on Television and the Radio

Advertisements on both television and radio can be seen by a large number of people thanks to broadcast and cable networks. The message of a brand can be communicated in a way that is both visual and audible through the use of these offline tactics.

2.3. Conventions and Commercial Exhibitions

Businesses have the opportunity to interact directly with potential consumers and partners when they participate in events, trade shows, and exhibits. This opens the door for in-person demonstrations as well as the development of relationships between the participating parties.

2.4. Patronage and Support

In the context of marketing and public relations, a sponsorship entails providing financial support to an event, a team, or an organization in exchange for branding and exposure. This tactic has the potential to improve both the visibility of the brand and its alignment with certain interests.

2.5. Direct and Televised Sales and Marketing

Direct sales and telemarketing tactics entail making direct contact with potential consumers via phone calls, door-to-door sales, or face-to-face interactions. These strategies can be used in conjunction with one another.

2.6. Advertisements in Public Places

Billboards, adverts displayed on public transportation, and signs erected in places with a lot of foot traffic are all examples of outdoor advertising. Because it offers exposure to pedestrians as well as drivers, it is useful for the promotion of local brands.

3. Combining Traditional and Digital Marketing Techniques

3.1. Branding That Is Consistent

It is quite important to keep the branding consistent across all marketing materials, whether they are online or offline. This includes making use of the same logo, color schemes, and messaging in order to establish a united brand identity.

3.2. Marketing Through Multiple Channels

Organizations may reach a larger audience and engage with clients on several fronts by developing multi-channel marketing campaigns that span both online and offline channels. These campaigns can help organizations create multi-channel marketing campaigns.

3.3. Monitoring and Statistical Analysis

The utilization of analytics tools can assist firms in determining the degree to which their offline and online marketing initiatives are producing the desired results. These discoveries can be used to adjust campaign strategies and make them more effective in the future.

3.4. Promotion in Other Venues

Utilizing one media to promote another is what is meant by the term "cross-promotion." For instance, driving online interaction can be accomplished by inserting a QR code in a print advertisement that links to a specific landing page on a website.

4. Distinctions between Traditional and Digital Methods of Marketing

4.1. Reaches and Intended Audiences

Online marketing has the capacity to reach an audience on a global scale, but offline marketing may have a reach that is more limited to a certain geographic area or demographic group.

4.2. Cost

When compared to some offline techniques, online marketing strategies typically offer a more cost-effective approach, particularly in regards to digital advertising. This is especially the case.

4.3. Interaction and Participation in Activities

Through the use of social media, comments, and other feedback methods, online marketing makes it possible to contact and engage with customers in real time. Offline techniques almost seldom involve this kind of real-time communication.

4.4. Capacity for Measurement

The effectiveness of an online marketing campaign may be measured in a variety of ways using the many tools that are available. When compared to online marketing, offline marketing can be more difficult to measure accurately.

4.5. The sense of touch

Offline marketing materials are tangible and can build a physical connection with the audience. Some examples of offline marketing materials include brochures and print advertisements. Digital media are important to online marketing.

5. The Effects That Marketing Have Both Online and Offline

5.1. Greater Public Awareness of the Brand

There is a correlation between greater brand visibility and awareness among target consumers and the use of both online and offline marketing methods.

5.2. Engagement of the Customer

Customer involvement is where online marketing really shines, but offline marketing methods can leave a more long-lasting impression because to the tangible products and face-to-face interactions they involve.

5.3. The Rates of Conversion

Because it is possible to target certain demographics with online marketing and monitor user activity, this type of marketing can result in higher conversion rates. It's possible that the conversion cycle for offline marketing will take longer.

5.4. Relationships with Customers

Building and sustaining relationships with customers is a valued activity that can be accomplished successfully through both online and offline marketing, with each method giving its own set of distinct advantages and opportunities for customization.

5.5. The Development of the Market

While online marketing enables market expansion on a worldwide scale and access to new audiences, offline marketing is typically used as a supplement to increase a company's share in a local market.

6. Obstacles to Overcoming When Trying to Strike a Balance Between Online and Offline Marketing

6.1. The Distribution of Resources

Businesses need to efficiently manage resources in order to strike a balance between their online and offline marketing efforts, while also taking into account the restrictions of their budgets and the returns they anticipate.

6.2. The Integration of Technology

The integration of offline and internet marketing technology can be a challenging process. It is essential, for the sake of providing a unified experience for the consumer, to guarantee the smooth flow of data across the two channels.

6.3. Accommodating Oneself to Current Market Trends

Continued research and a flexible approach to strategy formulation are required in order to successfully adapt to the ever-shifting marketing landscape and consumer behavior.

6.4. Calculating Return on Investment

Although it can be difficult, calculating the return on investment (ROI) for marketing initiatives that are carried out offline as well as online is an absolutely necessary step in the process of optimizing marketing budgets.

The use of both online and offline marketing methods is essential to the development of a complete marketing plan. To successfully communicate with their respective target audiences and advance their brands, companies need to find a middle ground between the two strategies outlined above. While online marketing makes it possible to engage clients in ways that are inexpensive, measurable, and highly engaging, offline marketing makes it possible to form connections with audiences that are tangible, customized, and long-lasting. Businesses are able to develop comprehensive marketing strategies that maximize their impact and reach by merging both techniques and exploiting the capabilities that are unique to each one. These campaigns are also able to react to shifting consumer behaviors and evolving market trends. Finding the correct balance between offline and online marketing that is congruent with the objectives of the company and the requirements of its target demographic is essential to the company's success.

7.3 Public-Private Partnerships in Tourism Promotion

Public-private partnerships (PPPs) play an important part in the promotion and development of the tourism industry. PPPs stimulate collaboration between government bodies and private firms to improve destination marketing and infrastructure, and they play an important role in the growth of the tourism sector. These collaborations capitalize on the advantages offered by both industries by pooling their respective resources, skills, and networks in order to develop a tourism ecosystem that is robust and environmentally responsible. PPPs have emerged as viable tools for generating economic growth, supporting community development, and assuring the long-term sustainability of tourism destinations within the sphere of tourism promotion.

The public and commercial sectors working together to promote tourism offers a number of benefits, one of the most important of which is the pooling of resources. Private companies contribute competence in areas such as marketing, technology, and customer service, while public institutions can provide access to public infrastructure, money, and regulatory support. This approach to working together enables the execution of complete advertising campaigns and the creation of tourism infrastructure that is beneficial to both tourists and the communities that are located in the surrounding area.

Marketing and Promotion: Public-private partnerships (PPPs) make it easier to develop sophisticated marketing and promotional campaigns that do an excellent job of showcasing a destination's distinctive amenities and activities. Destinations have the ability to build focused marketing activities that may reach an audience that is both diverse and global if they make use of the power of the government and the innovative techniques of the business sector. These efforts frequently promote the environmental, cultural, and historical attractions of an area in order to entice tourists and generate ongoing interest in the location as a destination.

Construction of Infrastructure Public-private partnerships play an important role in the construction of tourism infrastructure, which may include transportation networks, hotel facilities, and recreational activities. These agreements can make it easier to create new airports, highways, and public transportation systems, which will ultimately make tourism sites more accessible to visitors. In addition, partnerships in the hotel and hospitality industry can result in the creation of accommodations of a high quality that are able to fulfill the requirements and requirements of a wide variety of traveler segments.

Activities That Are Sustainable Public-private partnerships (PPPs) in tourist marketing frequently place an emphasis on tourism activities that are sustainable and responsible. Partnerships can contribute to the preservation of cultural heritage, the conservation of natural resources, and the promotion of eco-friendly tourism activities if they include sustainable initiatives into the creation of infrastructure and marketing campaigns.

This strategy not only ensures the continued profitability of tourist attractions but also encourages a beneficial impact on the environment and the community, which is to the advantage of both visitors and the residents of the surrounding area.

Community Engagement Through public-private partnerships, we may encourage greater levels of community engagement and participation in tourism marketing initiatives. Residents are more likely to feel a feeling of ownership and pride when they are given the opportunity to participate in tourism-related activities and are given a voice in the decision-making processes that affect their community through public-private partnerships (PPPs). This all-inclusive strategy has the potential to result in the maintenance of local culture and traditions, the generation of employment possibilities, and the general economic empowerment of local populations.

Sharing of Risks: Public-private partnerships (PPPs) make it possible for the public and private sectors to share the risks associated with large-scale tourist projects, which helps to reduce the related financial burdens. Both sides are able to navigate uncertainty more successfully when the risks and duties are shared, which ultimately leads to the successful implementation of tourism promotion activities and infrastructure development projects.

In general, public-private partnerships in tourist marketing are an essential component in establishing an environment that is favorable to the continued growth of sustainable tourism. These collaborations may create economic growth, conserve cultural heritage, and foster responsible tourist practices by combining the strengths of the public sector and the private sector. This ensures the long-term success and resilience of tourism destinations all over the world.

Chapter 8

The Role of Government

The obligations that fall under the purview of the government in a society are many, spanning the gamut from the upkeep of law and order to the promotion of economic growth, the provision of basic services, and the protection of the welfare of its own population. This all-encompassing investigation will dig into the multidimensional role that government plays in society, exploring its activities, responsibilities, and the impact it has on a variety of sectors of society.

1. **The Opening Statements**
   The institution of government, in all of its myriad permutations and tiers, is essential to the functioning of human society. It is responsible for establishing a framework for the operation of the state and seeing to it that its residents enjoy a high standard of living. There are several basic domains in which governments are typically involved, despite the fact that the particular activities and responsibilities of governments might vary greatly from one nation and political system to another.

2. The Roles That the Government Plays in Society

2.1. The Role of the Legislative

Making new laws and getting existing ones passed is the job of the legislative branch of the government. This process involves the formation of rules and regulations that control different parts of society, ranging from criminal justice and taxation to health and education. These statutes and regulations can be found in the United States Code. Legislative bodies are made up of representatives that have been elected to serve and are responsible for debating, drafting, and voting on proposed laws.

2.2. Functions of the Executive

It is the job of the executive arm of the government to put laws into effect and ensure that they are followed. This involves the management of governmental agencies, the conduct of law enforcement and international relations, as well as the implementation of various policies and initiatives.

2.3. The Role of the Judiciary

The judicial branch of the government is responsible for interpreting the laws and ensuring that they are applied in a manner that is both fair and just. Courts are responsible for settling disputes, providing interpretation of the constitution, and making decisions that establish new standards in the law. The rule of law relies heavily on the impartial decisions made by judges and juries.

2.4. The Function of Regulation

It is the role of numerous government organizations and bodies to regulate various businesses and sectors, such as the healthcare industry, the financial industry, and the environmental protection industry. Regulations are meant to establish standards, ensure compliance with those standards, and address concerns relating to public interest, fairness, and safety.

2.5. Defense and the Protection of the Nation

One of the primary responsibilities of the government is to safeguard the country against assaults from foreign enemies. For the purpose of preserving national security as well as good relations with other nations, governments are responsible for maintaining armed forces, intelligence agencies, and diplomatic services.

2.6. Services to the Public

Public services such as education, healthcare, transportation, and utility provision are among
the many that are made available to residents by their respective governments. These services, which are crucial for the health and well-being of residents as well as the quality of life they lead, are frequently financed by taxation.

2.7. The Regulation of the Economy

The function of the government in economic regulation includes the monitoring of markets, the promotion of equitable competition, and the elimination of monopolistic business practices. The involvement of the government may be undertaken with the purpose of safeguarding workers, consumers, and the environment.

2.8. Social Assistance and Welfare Services

Welfare and social service programs are often enacted by governments as a means of providing assistance to vulnerable and disadvantaged demographic groups. Included in these programs are benefits for unemployed individuals, assistance with food and housing, support for housing, and medical services.

3. The Duties That Come With Being in Government

3.1. Safeguarding Individual Liberties and Rights

It is the government's primary duty to safeguard the civil liberties and legal entitlements of its subjects at all times. These rights include the freedom to speak one's mind, practice one's religion, congregate with others, and have access to due process. Additionally, governments are responsible for preventing prejudice and protecting the rights of minority groups.

3.2. Safety and Protection of the Public

The upkeep of law and order is a fundamental duty that falls squarely on the shoulders of the governing body. This includes maintaining the safety of citizens, preventing and addressing criminal activity, as well as defending individuals and property from harm.

3.3. Responsible Management of the Economy

The government plays an important part in the management of the economy, as well as in the promotion of economic growth and the reduction of economic inequality. This task frequently includes the formulation of fiscal and monetary policies, as well as the administration of taxation and the regulation of financial markets.

3.4. Education and the Health of the Public

It is the duty of the government to provide services related to public health, such as the prevention of diseases, the administration of immunization programs, and access to medical treatment. Additionally, it is accountable for funding educational institutions and ensuring that all students have access to high-quality education.

3.5. The Construction of Infrastructure

The construction and upkeep of fundamental aspects of the physical environment, including but not limited to roads, bridges, and other forms of transportation as well as utility networks, falls within the purview of the nation's many governments. These infrastructure projects are essential for the growth of the economy and for improving people's quality of life.

3.6 International Affair and Relations

As the nation's representatives on the international stage, governments engage in diplomacy and other forms of international relations. They also keep up their diplomatic ties and engage in international organizations in addition to negotiating international agreements.

3.7. The Protection of the Environment

The government is taking on an increasing amount of responsibility for environmental preservation. This involves tackling concerns relating to climate change, regulating pollution, and protecting natural resources.

3.8. Response to Emergencies and Management of Disasters

In the phases of catastrophe preparedness, response, and recovery, governments play an essential role. This obligation encompasses the coordination of emergency services, the provision of aid to communities that have been impacted, and the maintenance of public safety during times of crisis.

4. The Repercussions of the Government

4.1. The Effect on the Economy

The economic climate is strongly influenced by the policies and choices made by the government. Economic expansion, price levels, and job opportunities are all susceptible to the effects of government expenditure, fiscal and monetary policies, and tax rules. The government has the ability to step in during times of economic turmoil to help stabilize markets and protect the populace.

4.2. The Effect on Society

The role that the government plays in the formation of the social fabric of society is an extremely important one. It has the potential to have an effect on education, healthcare, and social services, which in turn can have an effect on the residents' well-being and quality of life. In addition, the policies of the government regarding topics such as marriage equality, discrimination, and immigration can have an effect on the norms and perspectives of society.

4.3. The Effect on Politics

The forms and functions of a country's government are essential components of the political landscape of that nation. The democratic process as well as the power dynamics inside a society are impacted by political parties and institutions of government as well as elections.

4.4. The Impact on the Environment

Policies and restrictions enacted by governments have a significant bearing on the quality of the natural environment. Environmental sustainability and the protection of natural resources are both susceptible to being influenced by regulations pertaining to emissions, land use, and conservation efforts.

4.5. The Impact on Culture

The level of assistance provided by the government for the arts, culture, and historical preservation can have a considerable effect on the culture. A vibrant cultural identity can be fostered by providing financial support for cultural institutions such as museums, cultural activities, and historical preservation.

4.6. The Effect on Health

The government plays an active role in many aspects of public health, including the regulation of medical professionals and the coordination of response efforts during public health crises. Campaigns for public health and regulations placed on drugs such as smoke and alcohol are two more ways in which it is possible for this factor to impact health behaviors.

4.7. Impact on the World

The decisions that governments make regarding issues of international trade, politics, and diplomatic ties can have repercussions on a worldwide scale. A nation's place in the global community can be shaped in part by its involvement in international organizations, efforts to maintain peace, and the provision of humanitarian aid.

5. Obstacles Facing the Government

5.1. Bribery and Kickbacks

Worldwide, governments are struggling with the problem of endemic corruption. It reduces the public's trust in the government, causes a diversion of resources, and makes it more difficult for the government to carry out its duties.

5.2. The Administrative Structure

The delivery of public services can be slowed down and made

more difficult when bureaucratic inefficiencies and unnecessary red tape are present.

5.3. The Polarization of Politics

Polarization on political issues can result in stalemate, which makes it difficult for governments to make choices and carry out their plans.

5.4. Restricted Access to Resources

The ability of the government to solve urgent problems and deliver necessary services might be hindered when resources, especially budgetary constraints, are in short supply.

6. The Path Forward for the Government

6.1. The Transformation of Digital Technology

The use of digital technology is revolutionizing the operations and services provided by the government. E-government projects are improving accessibility and efficiency, and data analytics are improving decision-making. Both of these trends are contributing to improved government performance.

6.2. International Difficulties

On the world arena, the role that governments play will continue to be influenced by global concerns such as climate change, pandemics, and international conflicts.

6.3. Creativity, Innovation, and Social Transformation

The government's response to new innovations and shifting social norms will be shaped by these factors. Adaptation and forward-thinking policies will be necessary in order to address issues such as automation and artificial intelligence, as well as shifting demographics.

6.4. Participation of the Citizens

Changes in the way governments connect with and respond to their constituents are being brought about by increased citizen participation, which is made possible by advances in technology and increased openness.

The function of government is complex and multi-faceted, and it is an indispensable component in the operation of societies all over the world. The role of the government in preserving order, fostering economic growth, and ensuring the well-being of its population is indispensable, as it is responsible for everything from the drafting and execution of laws to the delivery of necessary services and the defense of rights. However, governments are also faced with a variety of problems, including instances of corruption and bureaucracy, as well as limited resources and political divisiveness. As societies progress, governments are forced to change in order to solve newly surfacing problems, encourage innovation, and respond to international concerns. As the government works to continue playing its critical role in the modern world, the digital transformation, global concerns, innovation, and more public participation will all play a role in shaping the future of government.

8.1 Government Policies and Tourism

Many nations rely critically on the tourism industry because it makes large financial contributions to their economies and facilitates interactions between different cultures. The policies of the government have a significant impact on the tourism industry, having an effect on everything from the construction of infrastructure to marketing techniques and initiatives to promote environmental sustainability. This in-depth investigation investigates the impact that government policies have on the tourist industry, as well as the techniques that governments use and the issues they confront when managing such an important industry.

1. **The Opening Statements**

    Tourism is a dynamic and varied industry that involves a large range of activities, ranging from hospitality and transportation to cultural exchange and recreation. This vast range of activities is what makes tourism such an interesting and rewarding field to work in. It is essential for the government to play a part in the development of the tourism industry since it has the capacity to affect both the sector's expansion and its ability to remain viable.

The policies of the government offer the regulatory framework, financial assistance, and strategic direction that are important for the growth of the tourism industry. These regulations have a significant bearing on a variety of facets of the sector, including the infrastructure, marketing, and long-term viability of the business.

2. **The Effects of Government Programs and Regulations on Tourism**

   2.1. The Creation of Physical Infrastructure

   The development of tourism infrastructure is heavily impacted by the policies of the government. Increasing a location's accessibility and allure to tourists is possible through strategic investments in modes of transportation, roads, and airports, as well as public facilities. The quality of the experience that tourists have as a whole is enhanced by carefully planned infrastructure, which also helps the tourism sector expand.

   2.2. Advertising and Business Promotion

   Promotion and marketing of tourist attractions are frequently included in official government policy. The marketing of a country or territory to attract both local and international tourists is the responsibility of the country's or region's national tourism board or agency. Advertising campaigns, trade exhibitions, and other online marketing tactics are examples of the kind of initiatives that fall under this category.

   2.3. Regulation and Quality Assurance Standards

   The tourism industry is subject to government regulation to ensure safety, quality, and ethical business practices.

   The regulations include a wide range of topics, such as hotel safety standards and the licensing of tour operators. These regulations are designed to safeguard vacationers while also preserving the honor of the industry.

   2.4. Protection of the Environment and of Cultural Assets

   Tourism that is favorable to the environment and respectful of local cultures is becoming an increasingly pressing issue, and government regulations play a critical part in addressing this challenge. Responsible tourism, preservation of cultural assets, and conservation activities can all be encouraged through the implementation of policies.

2.5. Policies Regarding Immigration and Visas

Tourism is directly influenced by the policy of various governments regarding immigration and visas. It is possible for entry criteria, processing waits for visas, and other limitations to either encourage or discourage visitors from traveling to a certain location.

2.6. Stimulus to the Economy

During times of crisis, such as the COVID-19 epidemic, the policies of the government have the potential to provide an economic boost to the tourism industry. Businesses that are dependent on tourism may be assisted in surviving and regaining their footing through the use of interventions such as financial support, tax advantages, and subsidies.

3. Strategies Employed by the Government in Regards to Tourism Policy

3.1. Partnerships Between the Public and Private Sectors

When it comes to tourist policy, one of the most popular strategies involves collaboration between government bodies and the private sector. Tourism can benefit from public-private partnerships (PPPs), which play to the respective strengths of both the public and private sectors. These agreements frequently involve cooperative advertising efforts, the creation of infrastructure, and the implementation of environmentally friendly policies.

3.2. Branding of the Destination

Many national governments have begun to recognize the importance of destination branding in developing a distinct and alluring public persona for their nation or region. A clear and distinct representation of a brand's identity has the potential to both draw in vacationers and improve their overall experience.

3.3. Initiatives Regarding Environmental Sustainability

The concept of sustainability lies at the center of a significant number of official initiatives. Implementing policies that are beneficial to the environment, lending support to conservation efforts, and encouraging ethical tourism activities are all potential strategies.

3.4. Management of Emergencies

When dealing with catastrophes that have the potential to disrupt tourism, such as natural disasters, health crises, or political instability, having effective crisis management methods is absolutely essential. In order for governments to effectively respond to these kinds of crises, they need to have communication strategies and emergency response plans in place.

3.5. Participation in the Community

It is crucial to involve local communities in the process of formulating tourist policies and plans. Strategies may include providing assistance to community-based tourist efforts, fostering the growth of local companies, and defending the legal standing and cultural practices of indigenous peoples.

4. Obstacles to Be Confronted in Tourism Policy

4.1. Excessive Tourism

The overwhelming influx of tourists can put a burden on resources, cause harm to the

environment, and cause disruption to local people. This problem, known as "overtourism," is a serious obstacle for many places. It is a difficult challenge to mitigate the negative effects of overtourism while still preserving money from tourism.

4.2. Striking a Balance Between Economic and Environmental Objectives

Policies regarding tourism need to strike a balance between fostering economic growth and protecting the environment. Finding this balance can be difficult since there are instances when commercial interests and conservation initiatives are in direct opposition to one another.

4.3. The Creation of Physical Infrastructure

Investing in tourism infrastructure is essential, but if it is not carefully controlled, it can also result in excessive development and the destruction of the surrounding ecosystem. It is a typical difficulty to find a balance between the demand for infrastructure and sustainable practices.

4.4. Management of Emergencies

Policies pertaining to tourism need to be flexible in order to efficiently manage unforeseen crises like pandemics or natural disasters. The development of comprehensive plans for crisis management and the maintenance of flexibility are both crucial.

5. Evolving Patterns and Cutting-Edge Developments in Tourism Policy

5.1. Responsible Travel and Tourism

The importance of environmentally responsible travel and tourism is rising, and as a result, government initiatives are putting a greater emphasis on sustainable tourism practices, responsible vacationing, and environmental protection.

5.2. The Transformation of Digital Technology

The tourism industry is undergoing a transformation due to the rise of digital technology, which can be seen in everything from online marketing to smartphone apps that improve the experience of tourists. These changes are being adapted to by governments, and technological advancements are being used to improve tourist services.

5.3. Intercultural Communication

The exchange of cultures is an essential component of tourism, and governments are making efforts to encourage genuine cultural encounters that are respectful of the traditions and legacy of local communities.

5.4. Concerning the Health and Safety

The COVID-19 epidemic has brought to light the significance of health and safety regulations within the tourism industry. Health procedures, travel restrictions, and vaccination measures are being implemented by governments as a means of protecting both visitors and permanent citizens.

Policies enacted by governments have a significant impact on the tourist sector, including the construction of infrastructure, marketing techniques, measures to preserve the natural environment, and activities designed to stimulate the economy. The effects of these policies can be seen in many different aspects of society, including the growth of the economy, the dissemination of cultural traditions, and the protection of the natural environment. Despite the fact that tourism brings both opportunities and challenges, the landscape of tourist policy is currently being reshaped thanks to novel methods and rising trends. As conditions continue to shift, governments play an increasingly important part in assuring the continued expansion and viability of the tourism industry, promoting the health and happiness of their own residents, and cultivating travel experiences that are both responsible and memorable for tourists.

8.2 Regulation and Oversight

Regulation and monitoring are basic components of modern governance. They play an essential part in the upkeep of order, the guarantee of fairness, the defense of public interests, and the development of a society that is stable and affluent. These methods are utilized in a diverse range of industries, ranging from the financial and healthcare industries to those concerned with environmental protection and consumer rights. This in-depth investigation dives at the significance of regulation and monitoring, as well as their application, the obstacles they face, and the advantages they provide to societies and economies.

1. **The Opening Statements**
   The rules, laws, and other procedures that are used by governments and other relevant authorities to monitor, regulate, and

exert influence over many elements of society and the economy are referred to collectively as regulation and oversight. These measures strive to ensure that activities, products, and services comply with set standards and contribute to the well-being of a society. They serve as a counterbalance to individual and corporate interests, and their purpose is to ensure that these interests are met.

2. **The Importance of Regulation and Supervision in Today's World**

   2.1. The Safeguarding of the Public Interest

   The purpose of regulation and oversight is to safeguard the public's best interests. They make sure that basic services like healthcare, transportation, and education are given in a fair and secure manner to everyone who needs them. In addition, they protect customers from potentially hazardous items, dishonest business activities, and unequal levels of competition.

   2.2. The Stability of the Market

   In the framework of the economy, regulation and oversight play an important role in helping to maintain market stability. These measures promote economic growth and defend against systemic crises by limiting monopolies, ensuring fair competition, and regulating financial institutions respectively.

   2.3. Protection of the Natural Environment

   Regulation and control of the environment are absolutely necessary for the preservation of
   natural resources, the protection of ecosystems, and the attenuation of the effects of pollution and climate change. These actions are designed to achieve a compromise between the need for economic growth and the preservation of the environment.

   2.4. Safety of the Public

   The level of public safety can be significantly improved by the use of regulation and oversight.
   Regulations establish and enforce safety standards in fields such as food and drug safety, transportation, and construction, with

the goals of reducing the occurrence of accidents and protecting public health.

2.5. Conduct That Is Both Ethical And Legal

Both the public and commercial sectors can benefit from increased ethical and legal behavior if regulations and oversight are implemented. These measures defend against unethical behavior and fraud and corruption by establishing explicit norms and holding entities accountable for violations of those rules.

3. The Institution of Regulatory and Supervisory Measures

3.1. The Drafting of Laws and Regulations

Legislation and the creation of regulations are at the core of the regulatory process. Within a particular market or industry, governmental bodies, agencies, and authorities are responsible for drafting, reviewing, and enforcing the rules and laws that define the standards, requirements, and boundaries.

3.2. Supervision and Administration of Sanctions

The components of oversight that are most important are monitoring and enforcement. Compliance with regulations is monitored by regulatory agencies and authorities, who check on firms, organizations, and individuals to verify that they are adhering to the requirements that have been set. This process frequently includes audits, inspections, and sanctions for those who do not comply with the regulations.

3.3. Obligation to Comply and Reporting

It is common practice to require regulated organizations to report on their actions and

demonstrate that they are in compliance with applicable legislation. This information is necessary for oversight and can be put to use to evaluate performance, find solutions to problems, and make decisions based on accurate data.

3.4. Do Your Homework and Perform an Audit

The regulatory and supervisory processes are data-driven. Data analysis is used by government agencies and research groups to determine the effects of regulations, keep an eye on trends, and arrive at judgments based on facts in order to continuously enhance regulatory and oversight processes.

3.5. Engagement with the Public and Advocacy

Participation from the public is an absolutely necessary component of regulatory and supervisory processes, particularly in situations in which regulations have an effect either on the populace as a whole or on certain interest groups. Stakeholders are given the opportunity to engage in the regulatory process and give voice to their concerns through the use of feedback systems, public consultations, and lobbying initiatives.

4. **Obstacles Facing Regulatory and Supervisory Bodies**

   4.1. Capture of the Regulatory System

The phenomenon known as regulatory capture takes place when the regulatory agencies that are supposed to regulate certain organizations become unduly influenced by such organizations. This can result in looser regulations and less strict enforcement of those regulations.

4.2. Complicated Procedures and Red Tape

Regulations have the potential to become excessively complicated and bureaucratic, which makes complying with them difficult and expensive, particularly for smaller enterprises. The process of simplifying and rationalizing regulatory requirements is difficult.

4.3. Costs Related to Compliance

Businesses may incur additional expenses in order to comply with rules, which may have a negative impact on economic growth and innovation. It can be difficult to find a happy medium between economic competitiveness and government regulations.

4.4. Inadequate Access to Resources

The difficulty that regulatory organizations frequently experience in acquiring sufficient resources is one of the many factors that can reduce their efficiency. When there is not enough money available, there may not be enough monitoring, enforcement, or oversight.

4.5. The Impact of Globalization

Because of their worldwide nature, many different industries provide difficulties for the monitoring and regulation processes. The need for international collaboration and standardized practices is necessitated by the existence of transnational problems, such as those relating to international finance or the environment.

5. The Advantages of Regulatory and Supervisory Measures

5.1. Protection of the Consumer

Consumers are shielded against potentially harmful products, deceptive business tactics, and unfair competition thanks to regulations and oversight, which also ensures that customers may have faith in the goods and services they purchase.

5.2. The Stability of the Market

Markets that are properly regulated are more secure and less likely to experience financial instability, which is beneficial for economic expansion and investment.

5.3. Protection of the Natural Environment

Setting criteria for emissions, waste disposal, and resource management are all areas in which regulations and monitoring can be of assistance in addressing environmental concerns.

5.4. Safety of the Public

Regulations in fields such as healthcare, transportation, construction, and food safety, which aim to reduce the likelihood of accidents and health hazards, contribute to an increase in public safety.

5.5. Conduct That Is Both Ethical And Legal

Regulation and monitoring encourage moral and lawful conduct, which helps to uphold public trust and avoid unethical or fraudulent business activities.

6. New Developments and Breakthroughs in the Areas of Regulation and Oversight

6.1. Oversight That Is Driven by Technology

The development of new technologies makes it possible to exercise supervision in a manner that is both more efficient and more effective. In a variety of business sectors, monitoring and enforcing compliance with regulations is being accomplished with the use of technological innovations such as blockchain and data analytics.

6.2. Regulation of the Environment and Long-Term Sustainability

The ever-increasing emphasis placed on preserving the natural environment serves as a primary impetus for novel approaches to environmental control.

Across the world, governments are taking action to combat climate change, protect natural resources, and encourage the adoption of environmentally responsible behaviors.

6.3. Regulations Regarding Cybersecurity

Regulations are being introduced by nations to protect data and vital infrastructure from the growing number of cyberattacks that are being launched. Regulations on cybersecurity are designed to protect individuals' private information, as well as intellectual property and the nation's safety.

6.4. The Role of International Organizations

Greater international cooperation in the areas of regulation and monitoring is being prompted as a direct result of global concerns such as pandemics and climate change. Countries are collaborating to set standards, share information, and coordinate their efforts to solve these difficulties in order to find a solution.

In order for a community and an economy to operate efficiently, regulation and oversight are both necessary components. They encourage ethical and lawful behavior, preserve public safety, promote market stability, and safeguard public interests. They also protect public interests. Emerging trends and innovations are transforming the landscape of regulation and oversight. This is happening despite the fact that obstacles such as regulatory capture, complexity, and resource restrictions remain. Effective regulation and oversight will continue to play a crucial role in the development of a just, safe, and sustainable society even as governments adjust to meet the changing demands of society as well as the changing needs of the global economy.

8.3 Tourism Promotion Agencies

Tourism promotion agencies are essential organizations that are responsible with marketing and promoting locations in order to attract tourists, drive economic growth, and improve the overall experience of visitors. These organizations play an important part in highlighting the one-of-a-kind attractions, cultural history, and recreational activities that a location has to offer to visitors. This condensed review focuses on the functions and strategies of tourism promotion agencies, highlighting their significance in increasing tourism and cultivating awareness of destinations.

It is the responsibility of tourism promotion companies to provide all-encompassing marketing strategies that showcase the most important features and experiences of a particular location. These organizations frequently work along with local companies, hospitality services, and government institutions to establish successful promotional programs that are geared toward specific visitor demographics.

The goal of tourism promotion companies is to pique the interest of prospective tourists by using a mix of tried-and-true methods (such as traditional advertising), cutting-edge methods (such as digital marketing), and strategic alliances.

Building a solid brand identity for a location is one of the key responsibilities that fall on the shoulders of tourism promotion companies. These agencies are able to develop a one-of-a-kind and unforgettable image that resonates with potential tourists by drafting an engaging narrative that reflects the cultural, historical, and natural features of a site. This branding is essential to developing a unique identity for the destination that differentiates it from other similar options on the market.

In addition, tourism promotion agencies participate actively in social media and digital marketing initiatives in order to reach a more extensive audience. These agencies are able to efficiently target certain demographics and communicate with potential tourists in real time by leveraging a variety of internet platforms, such as social networking sites, travel blogs, and digital advertising. When trying to create a captivating and immersive digital experience for users, it is common practice to make use of content that is visually appealing, imagery that is visually appealing, and interactive storytelling.

In general, tourism marketing agencies play a crucial part in propelling the expansion of the tourism industry and boosting the economic well-being of their respective locations. These agencies assist to the overall success and exposure of a site by developing effective marketing campaigns, nurturing destination branding, and leveraging digital platforms. As a result, the location is able to attract and welcome a varied spectrum of tourists from across the world.

8.4 Taxation and Tourism

There are a lot of moving parts and complexities involved in the link between taxation and tourism. Taxation policies have the potential to generate significant money for governments, but they also have the potential to have an impact on the affordability and appeal of tourist destinations. It is essential to find a happy medium between taxation and the maintenance of sustainable tourism practices. During this conversation, we are going to talk about the different types of taxes that are levied on the tourism business, the effects that these taxes have on governments as well as on travelers, and the difficulties that arise when trying to sustain a vibrant tourism industry while still collecting the necessary money.

1. **The Opening Statements**

    Numerous nations derive a significant portion of their financial resources from tourism, making it an important contributor to economic expansion, employment, and earnings in foreign currencies. The tourist industry is frequently relied upon by governments as a source of tax revenue that may be used to pay public service and infrastructure development. However, careful consideration needs to be given to the taxation of the tourism industry in order to ensure that the industry continues to be competitive and continue to draw in tourists.

2. **The Different Methods of Taxation Used in the Tourism Sector**

2.1 Taxes on Accommodations

The tax on accommodation is one of the forms of taxation that is utilized most frequently in the tourism business. These fees are often added onto the total cost of a hotel room and might range widely from one place to the next. The funds that are collected from hotel taxes are frequently designated for use in the marketing of tourism, the construction of new infrastructure, or the provision of local services.

2.2. The Taxes on Purchases as well as the Value-Added Tax (VAT)

A wide variety of products and services, including those purchased by visitors, are subject to sales and value-added taxes (VAT). However, the overall cost of living and traveling to a location might be impacted by these taxes, which contribute to the general revenue of the government.

2.3 Taxes Applied to Vacationers

Certain locations require visitors to pay certain taxes, which may take the form of a flat rate per

night or a percentage of the overall cost of the vacation. These taxes can vary from location to location. These levies are typically put toward funding community services, environmental efforts, or infrastructure improvement projects.

2.4 Taxes Applicable to Air Travel

Taxes related to air travel are typically added to the price of airline tickets. These taxes may take the form of departure fees, passenger charges, or taxes related to aviation fuel. The airline sector is responsible for collecting these taxes, but they can have an impact on how much it costs to travel to a certain location.

3. **The Effects of Taxes on the Tourism Industry**

   3.1 The Expense of the Trip

   The overall cost of traveling to a location can go up if there is a high tax rate, particularly on things like lodging and transportation by air. This can be a turnoff for price-conscious tourists and have an effect on a destination's ability to compete.

   3.2. Behavior of Vacationers

   As a result of the high taxation, tourists may alter their behavior. They could choose to remain for a shorter period of time, go with a less expensive accommodation option, or go to a location that has a lower overall tax load.

   3.3. The Competitiveness of the Destination

   The taxation system of a destination can have an effect on how competitive it is. Countries that have lower tax rates may be able to attract a greater number of tourists as well as foreign investment, which would ultimately increase the tourism industry in those countries.

   3.4. The Generation of Revenue

   Governments bring in a considerable portion of their overall revenue from taxation. The funds that are earned from tourism-related taxes can be reinvested in tourism promotion, infrastructure development, and public service provision, all of which are to the benefit of inhabitants and visitors alike.

4. **Obstacles Facing Taxation and the Tourism Industry**

   4.1 Excessive levels of taxation

   Taxes that are too high might be off-putting to potential visitors, which in turn can slow the expansion of the tourism business. An excessive tax burden may also encourage tax fraud as well as the provision of unlicensed lodging services, both of which may compromise the standard of tourist activities as well as their level of safety.

4.2 The Absence of Openness and Transparency

Taxation systems that are difficult to understand and lack transparency can lead to misunderstanding and discourage tourism. A misunderstanding of the way taxes are structured can be a source of contention and discontent for taxpayers.

4.3. Avoidance of Taxes and the Informal Economy

There are several locations where the informal accommodation services provided through platforms such as Airbnb may circumvent the conventional procedures of tax collection. Traditional hospitality firms may find themselves at a competitive disadvantage as a result of this.

4.4. The Effect on the Communities Nearby

The effect that taxation has on the communities that are directly affected by it is an essential factor to take into account. The local populace should profit from taxes, and taxes should contribute to the overall economic health of the destination.

5. Maintaining a Healthy Balance

5.1. Taxation That Is Both Fair and Transparent

Taxation systems should strive to be both equitable and open to public scrutiny wherever possible. Tourists may find it easier to understand and absorb the tax burden if the policies governing taxes are transparent and consistent.

5.2. Investing in the Infrastructure of the Tourism Industry

It is important for governments to make investments in tourism infrastructure and services in order to make the taxes paid by tourists worthwhile. The provision of high-quality services and amenities can both help to justify taxation and improve the experience of tourists.

5.3. Working Together with the Business Community

It is absolutely necessary for governments and the tourism industry to work together. This cooperation can assist design tax policies that support the growth of industries, the preservation of the environment, and the marketing of destinations.

5.4. Methods for Environmentally Responsible Tourism

The principles of sustainable tourism should be encouraged by governments, and tax revenue should be used to safeguard both natural and cultural resources. This strategy has the potential to entice tourists who are conscientious about their actions and to keep the industry viable over the long run.

Taxation is a crucial part of the tourism business since it brings in cash for governments and enables them to provide essential public services and maintain necessary infrastructure.

However, in order to achieve a balance between the collection of money and the industry's continued viability, special consideration should be given to the influence that taxing has on tourism. Together, investments in infrastructure and environmentally responsible tourism practices, together with equitable and fair taxation, can assist to maintain a robust and competitive tourism sector that is beneficial to both governments and tourists. Ultimately, the goals of efficient taxation policies should be to improve the quality of the tourism experience as a whole and to assure the continued economic success of popular tourist sites.

Chapter 9

Challenges and Controversies

1. **The Opening Statements**
   The human experience is rife with adversity and controversy, which helps shape the terrain of the world and propels conversations about pressing problems that plague civilizations, nations, and the planet as a whole. These complicated problems can include intricate interactions between a wide variety of parties, and finding successful solutions to them requires nuanced approaches and creative problem-solving strategies. This all-encompassing investigation digs into a wide variety of global issues and debates, providing insights into the factors that led to their emergence, the effects they have had, and the potential solutions to these problems.
2. **Social Difficulties and Contentious Debates**
   2.1. Social Inequality and the Pursuit of Justice
   On a global scale, the existence of persistent social inequality continues to be a substantial source of difficulty. The persistence of problems such as income inequality, racial discrimination,

and gender inequality highlights the necessity of comprehensive policies that promote social justice and inclusivity.

2.2. Infractions Against Human Rights

Persistent violations of human rights, including instances of tyranny, persecution, and abuses at the systemic level, can be found in many different regions of the world. It is still a significant obstacle that calls for united efforts and lobbying on a worldwide scale to overcome in order to guarantee the protection and promotion of fundamental human rights.

2.3. Migration Problems and the Plight of Refugees

Both the nations that are taking in refugees and the international community as a whole are facing significant challenges as a direct result of the rising number of migrants and refugees who are fleeing war, poverty, and persecution. In order to effectively manage these humanitarian crises, it is essential to tackle the underlying problems that lead to people being displaced and to develop policies that facilitate migration.

2.4. Concerns Regarding the Public Health

Communities all throughout the world are feeling the effects of global public health concerns such as pandemics, infectious diseases, and lack of access to healthcare. It is essential to develop international collaboration in disease prevention and control efforts, as well as to ensure equal access to high-quality healthcare services, in order to effectively address these challenges.

3. Political Challenges and Controversies in the Third Section

3.1. Conflicts and Tensions in International Politics

There is still a substantial threat to the peace and stability of the world posed by long-standing geopolitical tensions and disputes between nations. For the sake of reducing the risks connected with these geopolitical difficulties, it is imperative that territorial conflicts be resolved, that diplomatic communication be fostered, and that multilateral cooperation be encouraged.

3.2. Concerns Regarding Democracy and Governance

In many parts of the world, problems with democratic governance, such as authoritarianism, electoral integrity, and corruption, continue to be widespread. It is essential, for the purpose of sustaining the foundations of democracy, to safeguard democratic institutions while also fostering governance structures that are transparent and accountable.

3.3. Extremism and Violent Activism

The proliferation of terrorist organizations and violent extremism poses a significant threat to the
safety of people all over the world. In order to effectively resist the propagation of violent beliefs, it is essential to put into action comprehensive counterterrorism measures, to promote social cohesiveness, and to address the underlying reasons of radicalization.

3.4. Dangers to Computer and Network Security

The prevalence of cyber threats, such as cyberattacks, data breaches, and online misinformation, is growing at an alarming rate, which presents substantial challenges to the nation's security and its digital infrastructure. It is absolutely necessary to improve cybersecurity measures, foster international cooperation, and encourage digital literacy in order to effectively confront these constantly shifting threats.

4. Economic Challenges and Debates

4.1 The Widespread Problem of Economic Disparity

Significant economic issues continue to be posed by the widening gap that exists between countries with high levels of wealth and those with low levels of wealth. In order to overcome the global economic inequities that exist, it is essential to put into practice economic policies that are inclusive, to encourage international trade agreements, and to promote sustainable development.

4.2. Climate Change and the Transition to a Sustainable Society

The detrimental effects of climate change, which include the degradation of the environment, the occurrence of natural disasters, and the loss of biodiversity, present enormous challenges to the sustainability of the global community. It is absolutely necessary, in order to reduce the negative effects of climate change, to put into action comprehensive climate action plans, to encourage measures that promote renewable energy, and to boost environmental conservation activities.

4.3. Economic Conflicts and Protectionist Measures

There has been a considerable increase in economic instability and interruptions in global commerce as a direct result of the emergence of trade wars and protectionist measures among states. It is essential to mitigate the risks associated with trade disputes by fostering open and transparent trade policies, advocating multilateral trade agreements, and promoting fair trading practices.

4.4. The Relationship Between Poverty and Economic Development

The enduring problem of poverty and underdevelopment across the globe continues to be a significant obstacle for a great number of countries. It is very necessary, in order to support inclusive and equitable growth, to put into action comprehensive programs for the reduction of poverty, to promote sustainable economic development efforts, and to address socioeconomic imbalances.

5. Environmental Issues That Are Creating Difficulties And Controversies

5.1. The Effects of Climate Change and the Degradation of the Environment

The ever-worsening effects of climate change, which include an increase in average global temperatures, more severe weather, and the loss of polar ice, pose substantial obstacles to the environmental sustainability movement.

The implementation of strong climate action legislation, the promotion of sustainable resource management, and the facilitation of environmental conservation initiatives are all necessary components of an effective climate change mitigation strategy.

5.2. The Depletion of Biodiversity and the Destruction of Habitat

Significant challenges are posed to ecosystems all over the world and the natural resources they contain as a result of the accelerating loss of biodiversity and degradation of habitats. It is absolutely necessary, in order to preserve biodiversity on a global scale, to put into action comprehensive biodiversity conservation measures, to encourage wildlife protection programs, and to support sustainable land management practices.

5.3. The Depletion of Natural Resources

The unsustainable extraction of natural resources such as water, minerals, and forests creates enormous obstacles for the administration of the world's resources. It is vital, in order to solve the problem of natural resource depletion, to encourage responsible resource extraction techniques, to put conservation measures into place, and to create sustainable consumption patterns.

5.4. Controlling Pollution and Disposing of Waste

The rising levels of pollution, which include air pollution, water contamination, and trash produced by plastics, present substantial challenges to both the general public's health and the long-term viability of the ecosystem. It is absolutely necessary, in order to address issues regarding global pollution, to put into action comprehensive pollution control measures, to encourage waste reduction initiatives, and to create environmental awareness and education.

When it comes to solving problems and resolving conflicts on a global scale, we need multidimensional approaches, international collaboration, and consistent efforts from a variety of stakeholders. It is possible for nations to work together to overcome these issues and construct a society that is more fair, secure, and environmentally sustainable if they address social inequities, promote democratic government, stimulate sustainable economic development, and implement comprehensive measures to conserve the environment. It is possible for societies to work toward the creation of a global community that is both more welcoming of diversity and more prosperous as a result of collective action and a commitment to the promotion of good change.

9.1 Over tourism and Its Consequences

The tourism industry is a significant economic driver, a medium for the sharing of cultural traditions, and a tool for fostering international understanding. However, as a result of the rising interconnectedness of the world, locations all over the world are now dealing with the unintended repercussions of having an excessive amount of tourists visit them. This in-depth investigation dives at the idea of overtourism, as well as its underlying causes and the far-reaching effects it has on locations, local communities, and the environment.

1. **The Opening Statements**

   Travel and tourism have been a driving force behind global economic expansion and have made it possible for people from different cultures to communicate with one another. However, the rise in tourism, particularly in some of the most famous sites throughout the world, has resulted in a phenomena known as "overtourism." This describes a situation in which the sheer number of tourists overwhelms the capacity of a location to deal with them. This has significant repercussions for the quality of life of local residents, as well as for the environment and the local cultures.

2. **What Exactly Is an Overtourism Scam?**

   Overtourism, also known as tourism congestion, can place when a location has an excessive amount of tourists, which leads to a variety of unfavorable outcomes. Overcrowding at popular locations, increased pollution, strain on local infrastructure, and a loss of cultural authenticity are some of the negative effects of tourism. In recent years, various factors have contributed to an increase in the severity of overtourism. These causes include the proliferation of low-cost travel options, low-cost airlines, and the widespread use of social media.

3. **The Foundational Factors Behind Excessive Tourism**

   3.1. Internationalization and Interconnectedness

   Because of advances in transportation and communications, as well as the general interconnection of the modern world, vacationing is now more accessible than it has ever been. As a direct consequence of this, locations that were once inaccessible and reserved for a select few are now teeming with tourists.

   3.2. Advertising and Public Relations

   The herd mentality that develops among tourists as a result of aggressive marketing campaigns conducted by travel companies, airlines, and destination management groups frequently concentrates on "must-see" locations. These kind of marketing efforts could result in concentrated influxes of tourists.

   3.3. Platforms for Online Reservations

   It is now much simpler for tourists to book their rooms and other travel services thanks to the spread of internet booking platforms. This has contributed to increases in the number of visitors.

   3.4. Tourism for Cruises

   The tourism industry that revolves around cruises is a key contributor to overtourism. Overcrowding occurs frequently at smaller ports and cities as a result of large cruise ships disgorging thousands of passengers in a short amount of time.

   3.5. Leases for a Short Amount of Time

   The proliferation of home-sharing websites like Airbnb has resulted in an increase of short-term rentals in residential districts, which has resulted in the displacement of long-term residents and altered the personality of these neighborhoods.

4. **The Repercussions of Excessive Tourism**

   4.1. The Impact on the Environment

   An excessive amount of tourists might have a negative impact on the natural world. Popular natural areas are more likely to experience deforestation, pollution, and other forms of degradation to their ecosystems. In addition, the carbon footprint of travel, particularly travel by air, is a contributor to the phenomenon of climate change.

4.2. The Disintegration of Cultures

The overuse of tourism can have a detrimental effect on the local culture and traditions. The emphasis placed on catering to visitor needs might result in the commercialization and commodification of traditional behaviors, which can compromise the traditions' genuineness.

4.3. Pressure Placed on the Infrastructure

The sheer number of tourists can put a burden on the local infrastructure, which can lead to problems with things like transportation, sewage systems, and waste management. This may cause residents' regular routines to become more difficult to manage.

4.4. The Increasing Cost of Living

The cost of life for locals might become more expensive as a direct result of tourism, making it increasingly difficult for inhabitants to afford housing and other essential services.

4.5. Unfavorable Experience for Vacationers

Even the tourists themselves can have a negative experience in congested areas, as they are forced to struggle with long lines, overloaded attractions, and a lack of true relationships with the local culture.

5. Possible Answers to the Problem of Overtourism

5.1. Plans for the Management of Destinations

In response to the issues posed by overtourism, a number of places are currently working to build comprehensive destination management plans. These ideas include setting capacity restrictions, educating visitors, and making upgrades to the infrastructure.

5.2. Taxes and Other Charges for Visitors

Some tourist sites have instituted taxes or fees on tourists in order to generate cash for the maintenance of local infrastructure and to better control the number of visitors.

5.3. Practices for a Sustainable Tourism Industry

The mitigation of tourism's negative effects on the environment can be aided by the promotion of sustainable tourism practices. This includes activities such as observing wildlife in a responsible manner, reducing trash, and increasing energy efficiency.

5.4. Participation in the Community

It is possible to develop a sense of ownership and prevent negative impacts by including local communities in decision-making processes and providing economic benefits to them as a result of tourism.

5.5. Rules and Regulations for Vacation Rentals

Some locations have begun to regulate or prohibit short-term rentals in an effort to preserve residential neighborhoods and to ensure that these places retain their unique personalities.

An urgent problem on a global scale, overtourism has a negative impact not just on tourist sites but also on local populations and the natural environment. Because of globalization and marketing, there has been an increase in the number of tourists, which has put a burden on the infrastructure, diminished the local culture, and caused damage to the environment. Comprehensive destination management, environmentally responsible tourist practices, active participation from local communities, and appropriate regulation are some of the potential solutions to the problem of overtourism.

By tackling the issue of overtourism, destinations will be able to find a middle ground between the economic benefits of tourism and the preservation of their distinctive natural and cultural heritage. In the end, the objective is to make certain that tourism continues to be a driver of constructive change and increased mutual comprehension, rather than a cause of disturbance and environmental degradation.

9.2 Balancing Economic Growth and Environmental Preservation

One of the most fundamental issues that the 21st century will face is figuring out how to balance the competing goals of fostering economic expansion and protecting the natural environment. Industrialization, urbanization, and the consumption of resources are three of the most common ways in which nations put enormous strain on their environments in their pursuit of prosperity. The maintenance of a healthy equilibrium between the advancement of economic activity and the protection of natural resources is a difficult and urgent matter. This in-depth investigation delves into the complexities of the delicate act of sustainability, illuminating the primary challenges, approaches, and developing tendencies that are associated with this important activity.

1. **The Opening Statements**

   The quest of economic expansion is an essential component of the advancement of humankind. People are able to improve their living standards, receive a higher quality education, and receive better medical treatment as economic development occurs, giving them opportunity to lead more prosperous lives. On the other hand, economic expansion frequently comes at the expense of the surrounding environment. Industrialization and urbanization have led to a number of negative side effects, including the exhaustion of natural resources, the discharge of pollutants, and the decimation of ecosystems.

   On the other hand, protecting the environment is absolutely necessary to ensure the continued health of both the planet and the people who live on it in the long run. It maintains biodiversity and the delicate ecological balance, as well as ensuring that the air, water, and soil are clean and fertile. To accomplish economic progress without sacrificing the integrity of the environment is a difficult challenge, but it is one that must be met.

2. **The Most Important Concerns**

   2.1. The Consumption of Resources

   Growth in the economy is frequently dependent on the extraction of natural resources, which can lead to the depletion of such resources and, in certain circumstances, irreparable damage. An over reliance on limited resources, such as fossil fuels and minerals, puts the availability of these resources in the hands of future generations in jeopardy.

2.2. Pollution and the Alteration of Climate

Both industrial activities and transportation are major contributors to environmental pollution, especially in the air and water. In addition, the emissions of greenhouse gases that result from the burning of fossil fuels are the principal driver of climate change, which in turn leads to an increase in the frequency and severity of extreme weather events.

2.3. Destruction of Forests and Other Habitats

The expansion of urban areas and agriculture have been responsible for the clearance of forests and the degradation of natural ecosystems, which has led to a loss of biodiversity and put many species in risk.

2.4. The Production of Waste

An expansion in the economy typically results in an increase in the generation of garbage, which may include materials that are toxic or that cannot be recycled. The proper administration and disposal of trash might offer difficulties for the environment.

2.5. The Scarcity of Resources and the Volatility of Prices

Because to overexploitation, resources are becoming scarcer, which might cause the prices of those resources to become more unpredictable. This can result in instability in the economy as well as societal upheaval.

3. The Methods for Striking a Balance Between Development and Conservation

3.1. The Development of a Sustainable World

A primary goal of sustainable development is to satisfy the requirements of the here and now without jeopardizing the capacity of future generations to do the same for themselves. It places an emphasis on economic expansion that takes into account the economic, social, and environmental components.

3.2. Innovation and Technologies That Are Environmentally Friendly

The use of resources, pollution, and waste can all be cut down by businesses adopting environmentally friendly technologies and sustainable business practices. Renewable energy sources, energy-efficient technology, and sustainable agricultural methods are some of the technologies that fall under this category.

3.3. Policy Frameworks and Regulatory Requirements

The implementation of legislation, standards, and incentives that encourage responsible resource management and pollution reduction is one of the most important roles that governments can play in striking a healthy balance between economic growth and environmental preservation.

3.4. Evaluations of the Effects of Human Activities on the Environment (EIA)

An environmental impact assessment, or EIA, is a procedure that evaluates the potential effects of a proposed action or project on the surrounding environment. It assists in identifying potential consequences on the environment and offers suggestions for mitigating those impacts.

3.5. Methods That Are Based On Ecosystems

The conservation of natural resources and biodiversity may be served more effectively by focusing on the preservation of entire ecosystems as opposed to single species or regions. The health of ecosystems and the benefits they offer to humans are given the utmost importance by these approaches.

4. The Importance of Collaborative Efforts Across National Boundaries

4.1 The Agreement Reached in Paris

The landmark worldwide deal known as the Paris Agreement aims to hold the increase in the earth's average temperature to far below 2 degrees Celsius above its pre-industrial levels. It promotes governments to cut emissions of greenhouse gases and migrate to economies with lower levels of carbon output.

4.2. The 2030 Agenda for Sustainable Development (also known as the SDGs)

The Sustainable Development Goals (SDGs) outlined by the United Nations comprise a number of objectives with the overarching objectives of eradicating global poverty, preserving the environment, and fostering inclusive prosperity. These goals, in particular Goal 13 (Climate Action) and Goal 15 (Life on Land), highlight the significance of striking a balance between the expansion of the economy and the maintenance of the natural environment.

4.3. The Intergovernmental Panel on Climate Change (IPCC) has issued their latest report

The Intergovernmental Panel on Climate Change (IPCC) is a scientific group that was founded by the United Nations to evaluate the scientific research associated with climate change. Its reports educate both policymakers and the general public about the current status of climate research as well as potential measures for climate change mitigation.

4.4. Economic Partnership Agreements That Contain Environmental Provisions

Environmental elements are increasingly included in a significant number of trade agreements. These provisions encourage environmentally responsible business activities and discourage the degradation of the environment.

5. Obstacles and Rebuttals to Criticisms

5.1. Economic Concerns with a Short-Term Perspective

The pursuit of economic interests in the short term can frequently eclipse worries about the environment in the long run. This can lead to the exploitation of natural resources with insufficient thought given to whether or not they will be sustainable.

5.2. Uneven Distribution of Wealth

There is a disparity in the distribution of the benefits of economic progress, which might exacerbate existing environmental issues. Communities that are economically challenged may be more likely to face the brunt of environmental degradation, despite the fact that wealthier populations leave a larger environmental imprint.

5.3. The Boundaries of Current Technology

There is a possibility that not all countries will be able to finance completely developed or fully developed versions of certain environmentally friendly technologies, which will hamper their capacity to shift to more sustainable practices.

5.4. Resistance to the Rules and Regulations

Some companies and political interests may be opposed to legislation and programs that encourage environmental preservation on the grounds that they restrict economic expansion.

6. New Developments and Potential Opportunities

6.1. The Economy Based on Circularity

The goal of a circular economy is to produce a sustainable closed-loop system by reducing waste, maximizing the use of existing resources, and recycling whatever can be recycled.

6.2. Transition to Renewable Energy Sources

The shift away from fossil fuels and toward renewable energy sources such as solar, wind, and hydropower is gaining steam and will eventually result in a smaller carbon footprint associated with the production of energy.

6.3. Ecotourism and Other Forms of Responsible Travel

The discipline of ecotourism, which places an emphasis on ethical and environmentally conscious vacationing, is gaining in popularity. More and more frequently, vacationers are looking for vacation spots as well as places to stay that place a priority on protecting the environment.

6.4. The Promotion of Economic Development through Conservation

The idea that environmental protection can be a driver of economic expansion is getting more and more popularity. It is possible to make income from tourism and the utilization of resources in a sustainable manner with investments in protected areas and conservation programs.

Finding a happy medium between expanding the economy and also protecting the natural world is a complex and ever-evolving task that calls for the concerted efforts of individuals, businesses, and governments working together. In today's world, achieving sustainability requires an economic development strategy that recognizes and honors the limits of the earth while also taking into account the needs of next generations. Societies can work toward the goal of achieving a harmonious coexistence of economic prosperity and environmental integrity by cultivating a profound dedication to the responsible use of natural resources, the development of environmentally friendly technology, and cooperation across international borders.

9.3 Community Conflicts and Tourism

Tourism can present communities with both opportunities and challenges. Although it has the potential to bring about economic gains and chances for cultural interaction, it also has the potential to lead to conflicts and issues that have an impact on the lives of residents of the surrounding area. This essay explores the complicated relationship between community conflicts and tourism, shedding light on the most important problems, what may be causing them, and some possible remedies.

1. **The Opening Statements**

    It is common practice to view tourism as a potential source of income, employment, and cultural exchange for communities all over the world. On the other hand, it may also bring up a variety of difficulties, some of which may result in disputes between tourists and local inhabitants. These disputes can be caused by a wide variety of factors, including but not limited to overcrowding, rising expenses of living, cultural tensions, and environmental deterioration.

2. **Principal Concerns**

   2.1. Overcrowding and Traffic Snarls and Jams

   It is possible for popular tourist attractions to become overcrowded, which can cause traffic jams and other inconveniences for inhabitants as well as tourists. It may be challenging for local residents to navigate their own neighborhoods, and the experience may not be enjoyable for tourists owing to the increased foot traffic at popular locations.

   2.2. The Cost of Housing and the Overall Cost of Living

   Real estate prices have the potential to rise in certain locations due to increased demand for homes from tourists, particularly through online marketplaces such as Airbnb. This can make it difficult for local inhabitants to obtain home that is within their price range, which may contribute to the process of gentrification.

   2.3. Conflicts Between Cultures

   It is possible for visitors to accidentally violate the cultural norms of the area, which might heighten the level of friction between tourists and locals. Dissimilarities in attire, conduct, or expectations can all contribute to these types of cultural collisions.

   2.4. The Impact on the Environment

   Tourism can put a pressure on the ecosystems of a region and contribute to the degradation of the environment. This is especially true in regions that have delicate ecosystems, such as coastal areas and natural parks, where there are less resources available.

   2.5 Economic Inequalities and Inequities

   It's possible for tourism to make economic gaps in a town even wider. It's possible that some residents won't benefit economically from tourism even though there are jobs tied to the industry.

3. The Roots of Conflicts Within Communities

3.1. Unregulated Markets and Businesses

In many locations, the absence of regulation in the tourism industry can make existing tensions even worse. It is possible that issues relating to overcrowding, housing, and environmental effect will not be addressed if there is not adequate oversight.

3.2. A Lack of Sensitivity to the Culture of the Area

It's possible that tourists and businesses that cater to tourists aren't always aware of the local culture and values, which might result in cultural misunderstandings and problems.

3.3. Inadequate Facilities and Equipment

There is a possibility that certain villages do not possess the necessary infrastructure to manage the surge of tourists. It's possible that infrastructure like roads, public transportation, and sanitation facilities won't be able to keep up with the demand.

3.4. Advertising and Public Relations

It is possible that aggressive marketing and promotion techniques would result in an overwhelming influx of tourists, which will then lead to confrontations as a result of a lack of preparation.

4. Suggestions for Possible Solutions

4.1. Participation in the Community

Participation from the local population in the planning and development of tourism can be an effective tool for resolving problems. Their insights can help influence the formulation of policies and programs that strike a healthy balance between the needs of locals and tourists.

4.2. Zoning and Regulatory Measures

The implementation of rules and zoning ordinances that address concerns such as housing and

overcrowding can assist regulate the influence that tourism has on a community by reducing the negative effects of tourism.

4.3. Methods of Maintaining a Sustainable Tourist Industry

It is possible to reduce the negative effects of tourism on the surrounding ecosystem by promoting sustainable tourist behaviors. Some examples of these practices are responsible wildlife viewing, waste minimization, and energy efficiency.

4.4. Programs for Raising Cultural Awareness

Programs that raise tourists' cultural sensitivity can contribute to the reduction of cultural divides and the resolution of cultural disputes. Etiquette and local traditions are topics that can be included in these seminars for tourists.

4.5. Taxes and Other Fees Assessed to Vacationers

The imposition of various taxes and levies on tourists has the potential to create cash that may be put back into the community, so contributing to the reduction of expenditures incurred as a result of tourism.

Community conflicts and tourism are inextricably interwoven, and it is imperative that community conflicts be resolved if the tourism business is to remain viable and local residents are to enjoy a high quality of life. Communities are able to strike a balance between the economic benefits of tourism and the preservation of their cultural heritage, environment, and quality of life if they adopt a holistic approach that incorporates community engagement, regulation, and sustainable practices. This approach is necessary in order to achieve this balance. The creation of a healthy cohabitation that is to the advantage of all parties involved and that assures the continued economic viability of tourist sites is the objective of this project.

9.4 The Future of Tourism: Virtual Tourism and Beyond

Tourism has been an essential component of human culture and social interaction for many years, providing individuals with the opportunity to discover new locations, engage with people from other cultures, and make experiences that will last a lifetime. However, as a result of technology breakthroughs and altering societal patterns, the ways in which we travel and see the globe are undergoing a period of fast change. The future of tourism is investigated in this article, with a specific emphasis placed on virtual tourism as well as other developing trends that are transforming the way that people travel and discover new parts of the world.

1. **The Opening Statements**

   The tourism sector has historically revolved around physical travel, which enables people to visit far-flung areas and experience the distinctive characteristics of those places. On the other hand, new breakthroughs in technology, shifting preferences among consumers, and growing worries about the environment are all spurring a transition in the way people travel and interact with tourism. The idea of travel itself is being redefined, and the scope of what might be discovered is being expanded as a result of several new developments, including virtual tourism. This paper investigates the future of tourism, with a particular focus on virtual tourism as well as the larger implications of recent technological advancements in the industry.
2. **Tourism in the Digital Age: The Next Big Thing**

2.1. What Is Meant by the Term "Virtual Tourism"?

The term "virtual tourism," which is often referred to as "virtual travel" or "digital tourism," describes the practice of utilizing digital technology in order to discover and experience locations, cultures, and attractions without actually being present at the area.

It provides a way to visit places and take part in activities that were traditionally restricted to physically traveling to those locations and participating in those activities.

2.2. Virtual Reality (VR) and Augmented Reality (AR) are both types of mixed reality.

Recent developments in virtual reality (VR) and augmented reality (AR) technologies have paved the way for the establishment of virtual tourism. Virtual reality (VR) allows users to have an experience that is as realistic as possible by having them don headsets and be transported to digital recreations of real-world locations. On the other hand, augmented reality (AR) superimposes digital information and experiences onto the physical world using devices such as smartphones or glasses that display AR.

2.3. Principal Characteristics of Online Tourism

1. **Immersive Experiences:** Virtual tourism gives users the ability to explore locations by means of 360-degree films, interactive maps, and digital tours, thereby producing immersive experiences that closely match the experience of actual travel.
2. **Cultural Exchange:** This feature gives users the ability to interact with local cultures by participating in live cultural events, virtual language sessions, and virtual cookery classes.
3. **Accessibility:** People who have physical disabilities, financial restraints, or other limitations are able to discover the globe in ways that were previously inaccessible thanks to the advent of virtual tourism.
4. **Contribution to Efforts Towards Sustainability:** Virtual tourism can help contribute to efforts toward sustainability by minimizing the need for physical travel, which in turn reduces the carbon footprint connected with tourism.

III. The Possibilities Involved in Online Tourism
3.1. Improved Capacity for Pre-Trip Planning

When it comes to travel preparation, virtual tourism can be a very helpful tool. Before embarking on an actual trip, vacationers can virtually visit the locations of their choosing, gain access to information that was created by other users, and gain a better understanding of what to anticipate.

3.2. Mutual Sharing of Educational and Cultural Experiences

Students, as well as people who are learning for the rest of their lives, have the opportunity to become fully immersed in a variety of societies and time periods through the use of virtual tourism, which can be an effective instructional tool. It does this by exposing its users to a wide range of different languages, cultures, and practices, which in turn helps to promote international understanding.

3.3. Tourism That Is Sustainable

Because it lessens the toll that travel has on the environment, virtual tourism has the potential to play a big part in efforts to make tourism more sustainable. It inspires travelers to pick their places with care and may even result in a decrease in the amount of overtourism that occurs.

3.4. Economic Window of Opportunity

The proliferation of virtual tourism opens up doors for the development of innovative digital services, the production of immersive experiences, and the dissemination of original content. Within this burgeoning sector of the economy, opportunities await those who are enterprising enough to create original material.

IV. New Developments in the Tourism Industry

4.1. Travel That Is Both Responsible And Sustainable

More and more tourists are looking for environmentally friendly and socially responsible vacation options, with the goals of lowering their ecological footprint, giving back to the communities they visit, and safeguarding their natural and cultural heritage.

4.2. Tourism for Outdoor Activities and Extreme Activities

Travelers are increasingly looking for one-of-a-kind, off-the-beaten-path experiences, such as hiking, wildlife encounters, and extreme sports, which has led to an increase in the popularity of adventure and outdoor tourism.

4.3. Tourism Relating to Health and Wellness

The desire to improve one's health and well-being is leading an increasing number of tourists to look for vacation spots that have opportunities for rest and relaxation, such as yoga retreats, spa treatments, and other activities that boost both physical and mental well-being.

4.4. Tourism in the Culinary Arts

Travelers are increasingly interested in participating in culinary tourism, which includes exploring a variety of cuisines and food markets, as well as taking part in cooking lessons and other activities related to food.

4.5. Tourism in Outer Space

The idea of human travel into space is no longer limited to the realm of science fiction. Companies such as SpaceX and Blue Origin are making progress toward their goal of providing private persons with the opportunity to participate in commercial space flight.

V. Obstacles and Things to Take Into Account

5.1. Inequality in the Digital Age

Those who do not have access to digital technologies or internet connections that are fast may be unable to participate in virtual tourism, which would exacerbate existing digital divides.

5.2. Appropriation of Other Cultures

Because users may interact with cultural content without having a complete comprehension of its value, virtual tourism has the potential to unintentionally foster cultural appropriation if it is not managed with sensitivity.

5.3. Loss of Authenticity Due to Erosion

The growth of virtual experiences could result in a shallow comprehension of locations, which could potentially lessen the impact that travel has on one's ability to connect with their surroundings.

5.4. Displacement from One's Job

It is possible that jobs in traditional tourism sectors would be lost as a result of the growth of virtual tourism and automation within the business.

Technology, shifting consumer preferences, and environmental concerns are all factors that will play a role in reshaping the terrain of the future of tourism, which promises to be an exciting and dynamic era. The advent of immersive and interactive experiences made possible by virtual tourism is widening the definition of exploration while simultaneously opening up new frontiers for tourists. It is vital, however, to manage the ever-changing tourism business with care, taking into consideration the implications of digital inequality, cultural sensitivity, and the maintenance of authenticity.

In an ever-evolving world of travel and discovery, players in the tourism industry will need to be flexible and creative in order to navigate the opportunities and challenges that lie in the future of the industry.

Chapter 10

The Future of Tourist Dollars

1. **The Opening Statements**
   Each year, tourism results in revenue that is in the billions of dollars, making it a driving force in the world economy. Many nations and areas rely heavily on tourism as an important source of revenue since tourists spend a significant amount of money while they are there on a variety of different goods and services. The travel and tourism sector has seen tremendous change throughout the course of its history, and the years to come are likely to bring about even more adjustment as a result of developments in technology, evolving preferences among travelers, and ongoing difficulties on a worldwide scale. During this in-depth investigation, we will delve into the future of tourist dollars and investigate important trends, issues, and possibilities in the tourism sector.
2. **The Current Scenario in the Tourism Industry**
   2.1. The Importance of Tourism to the World Economy
   One of the major industries in the world, tourism is responsible for a sizeable portion of the world's gross domestic product

(GDP) and provides employment opportunities in a diverse range of industries, including hospitality, transportation, food service, and entertainment. It is an important contributor to the economic growth of a great number of countries.

2.2. Behavior of Vacationers

Changes are occurring in the preferences and behaviors of tourists. Travelers in the modern day place a higher value on experiences that are one of a kind and authentic, prioritize sustainability and eco-consciousness, and rely heavily on digital technology to plan and book their vacations.

2.3. Connectivity on a Global Scale

People are able to travel to more remote locations with greater ease as a result of advancements in transportation infrastructure, particularly in the form of better air travel networks and high-speed rail networks. The proliferation of mobile applications and online booking platforms has also contributed to an increase in international connectivity.

2.4. Locations of Tourist Attractions

There are many different places that benefit financially from tourism, ranging from well-known urban hubs to less accessible nature beauties. Tourism powerhouses include Paris, New York City, and Tokyo; nevertheless, rising locations in Asia, Africa, and South America are becoming increasingly appealing to travelers.

3. New Developments and Emerging Trends in the Tourism Industry

3.1. Responsible Travel and Tourism

The tourist sector is rapidly changing, and one of the primary drivers of this transition is sustainability. More and more tourists are looking for environmentally friendly places to visit and places to stay, and in response, businesses are beginning to implement environmentally conscious policies and procedures.

3.2. Travel With an Authentic Purpose

Travelers today are less interested in the conventional forms of sightseeing and more interested in having immersive and experiential vacations. Because of this tendency, activities such as culinary tours, adventure tourism, and cultural exchanges have become increasingly popular.

3.3. Wellness and the Tourism Industry in Health

The terms "health tourism" and "wellness tourism" are becoming increasingly common as an increasingly large number of vacationers are looking for places to go and activities to partake in that will improve both their physical and emotional well-being.

3.4. The Transformation of Digital Technology

With the growth of online booking platforms, mobile apps, and technologies like virtual reality (VR) and augmented reality (AR), the travel industry is undergoing a digital transition. These developments are influencing how vacationers plan their trips, what they do during their vacations, and how they talk about their experiences.

3.5. Tourism in Outer Space

Companies like SpaceX and Blue Origin are focused on developing commercial space travel, which is leading to the development of a new submarket: space tourism. This business, despite the fact that it is just starting off, has the potential to rethink the idea of tourist money in the future.

4. Obstacles Facing the Tourism Sector of the Economy

4.1. Excessive Visitation

Overtourism is a rising problem in popular areas, where high tourist numbers lead to congestion, increasing expenses of living, and environmental degradation. This problem is compounded by the fact that overtourism is a global phenomenon. Managing excessive tourism while preserving the health of the local economy presents a difficult challenge.

4.2. The Impact on the Environment

The carbon footprint left by tourism, which is primarily caused by air travel but also includes other means of transportation, is a contributor to climate change and the damage of the environment. To lessen the severity of these effects, sustainable behaviors are required.

4.3. Appropriation of Other Cultures and Lack of Respect

It's not uncommon for tourists to accidentally cause offense to the customs, rituals, and traditions of the area they're visiting. The task of finding a happy medium between cultural exchange and respect for one another is an ongoing one.

4.4. Inequality in the Digital Age

There are some areas and communities that do not have the same level of access to the digital tools and platforms that are essential to the operation of modern tourism. The unequal access to digital resources can stifle economic expansion in certain regions.

4.5. The Existence of Economic Inequalities

Tourism has the potential to generate economic possibilities; however, not all people of a community will necessarily share in the advantages of these chances. This can lead to differences in income as well as differences in standards of living.

5. Potential Career Paths Within the Tourism Industry

5.1. Methods That Are Environmentally Friendly

Not only do environmentally responsible tourism activities aid in the conservation of natural resources, but they also appeal to the expanding market of eco-conscious vacationers. The adoption of environmentally friendly practices can result in cost savings and a differentiated brand.

5.2. The Protection of Cultural Assets

Cultural preservation can be encouraged through responsible tourism by fostering the protection of cultural heritage and facilitating the transmission of local traditions and practices to tourists.

5.3. Recent Developments in Technology

The utilization of technology, such as virtual reality, augmented reality, and blockchain, has the potential to completely transform the travel and tourist business. These advancements provide opportunity for experiences that are more immersive, transactions that are more secure, and operations that are more efficient.

5.4. Tourism Relating to Health and Wellness

The sector for health and wellness tourism is one that is rapidly expanding and presents various potential for expansion. This trend presents an opportunity for destinations and businesses that cater to travelers interested in wellness to make money.

5.5. Tourism in Outer Space

The industry of space tourism is one that has a significant amount of untapped potential. It is possible that in the future, as technology improves and costs go down, this may become a sustainable enterprise, which will open up a new area for tourists and the collection of money.

6. The Projection of Revenue from Tourists

6.1. Augmented Reality and Virtual Vacations

It is expected that technologies such as virtual reality and augmented reality will continue to

promote the expansion of virtual tourism, which will enable tourists to discover new locations and activities without leaving the convenience of their own homes. In addition to generating new revenue sources for the industry, this can serve as a bridge for people who are physically unable to travel.

6.2. Cryptocurrency and the Use of Digital Wallets

There has been an uptick in the number of transactions conducted in the tourism sector using digital wallets and cryptocurrency. These technologies provide payment methods that are secure, efficient, and cost-effective. As a result, the costs associated with currency exchange may be reduced, and foreign transactions may be streamlined.

6.3. Tourism in Outer Space and Beyond

There is a possibility that in the not-too-distant future, private enterprises may compete to become the industry leaders in providing commercial space travel. This industry, despite the fact that it is just starting off, has the potential to introduce whole new options for the tourism industry and to rethink the concept of tourist dollars.

6.4. Tourism That Is Sustainable Becoming the Norm

As tourists grow increasingly conscientious of the influence they have on the environment, sustainable tourism techniques will continue to gain popularity. The economic benefits of catering to environmentally conscious tourists are expected to accrue to destination management organizations and enterprises who implement environmentally friendly business practices.

6.5. Experiences That Are Tailored To You And Individualized

The use of technology and data analytics will make it possible to create more individualized and customized travel experiences, which will adapt to the preferences and interests of each individual. This level of customization has the potential to increase consumer happiness, which in turn can lead to increased spending by tourists.

The tourism industry is undergoing tremendous changes, which will have a significant impact on future tourist spending. The travel industry is currently facing a number of difficulties and opportunities as a result of the way in which the globe is explored being reshaped by developments in technology and sustainability as well as the preferences of travelers. To ensure the continued expansion and vitality of the tourist industry over the long term, it is essential for governments, destination management organizations, and enterprises to adjust to these shifts, adopt methods that are environmentally friendly, and exploit breakthroughs in technology. They will be able to continue to promote responsible and immersive travel experiences for tourists all around the world by doing so, which will allow them to continue to capitalize on the economic power of tourist money.

10.1 Emerging Trends in Tourism

The tourism sector has always been dynamic, adjusting to new developments in technology, shifting preferences among travelers, and new circumstances throughout the world. Over the course of the past several years, the tourism industry has undergone substantial developments that are altering the way in which people travel and experience different locations. This essay investigates recent developments in the tourist industry and provides insights into the ways in which these developments are influencing the future of travel.

1. **The Opening Statements**
   The tourism industry is always moving forward, adapting to new social norms, technology developments, and environmental concerns. Travelers today are more varied and discerning than in the past, looking for one-of-a-kind experiences that go beyond the standard tourist attractions. As a result of these transformations, the tourism sector is embracing innovation, sustainability, and personalization in order to better serve the ever-evolving requirements of travelers. This essay provides a glimpse into the future of travel by analyzing developing trends in tourism and discussing those tendencies.
2. **Tourism That Is Sustainable**
   2.1. **What Is Meant by the Term "Sustainable Tourism"?**
   Sustainable tourism, sometimes known as responsible tourism, is an approach to vacationing that seeks to reduce the adverse effects of travel on local communities, as well as the environment, society, and culture, while emphasizing the positive effects on those communities and the environment. This movement emphasizes the need of preserving natural resources, safeguarding cultural legacy, and fostering ethical business practices across all sectors.
   2.2. **The Increase in the Number of Eco-Conscious Vacationers**
   Travelers are becoming increasingly interested in visiting areas and staying in lodgings that are conscious of their impact on the environment. This includes selecting environmentally friendly modes of transportation, supporting animal encounters that are

environmentally responsible, and decreasing their carbon footprint through the judicious use of travel options.

2.3. Providing Assistance to the Local Community

The inclusion of local residents in the decision-making process and a more equitable distribution
of the economic advantages generated by tourists are two key components of sustainable tourism, which both contribute to the growth of the local economy. This movement encourages community-based tourism efforts that provide genuine and all-encompassing experiences for visitors.

2.4. Certifications and standards

Certification systems, such as EarthCheck and Green Key, are gaining popularity as more and more visitors look for ways to validate that the decisions they are making are environmentally responsible. These programs encourage openness and responsibility within the travel and hospitality industry.

3. Travel with a Sense of Adventure

3.1. Beyond the Boundaries of Sightseeing

Experiences that go beyond the typical sightseeing are becoming an increasingly attractive option for today's vacationers. They are interested in having experiences that are interactive and immersive, which will help them to connect with the nature, history, and culture of the area.

3.2. Tourism in the Culinary Arts

The subfield of experience travel known as culinary tourism is becoming increasingly well-liked. Travelers are keen to try new cuisines, go to local food markets, and take part in cooking lessons and other activities linked to food when they are away from home.

3.3. Tourism for Adventurous Pursuits

Hiking, interacting with local wildlife, and participating in extreme sports are all examples of activities that fall under the category of adventure tourism. It is geared toward adventure-seeking tourists who are interested in exerting themselves in secluded and difficult settings.

3.4. Intercultural Communication

The surge in popularity of cultural exchange programs and language immersion courses provides tourists with the opportunity to learn about and participate in the customs and traditions of the communities in which they visit.

4. Tourism Related to Health and Wellness

4.1. What Is Meant When We Talk About Health And Wellness Tourism?

Traveling with the primary intention of improving one's physical, mental, and emotional well-being is what is known as "health and wellness tourism." People who travel want to go to places and have experiences that allow them to relax, such as spa treatments, yoga retreats, meditation centers, and fitness centers.

4.2. Travel with Contemplation

During their journeys, tourists are placing a greater emphasis on making time to disconnect from their devices, reduce their levels of stress, and care for themselves in general. This movement is characterized by activities such as meditation retreats, internet detoxes, and wellness-focused vacations.

4.3. Delicious and Nutritious Food

Consuming foods that are good for you is an essential part of health and wellness tourism.

Many vacationers are looking for destinations that provide farm-to-table, organic eating alternatives and culinary experiences that are centered on nutrition.

4.4. Health Spas and Relaxation Getaways

It is becoming increasingly common for vacationers to visit spas and wellness retreats, which provide opportunity to unwind, revitalize, and concentrate on both their physical and emotional well-being.

5. **The Evolution of Digital Technology**

   5.1. Platforms for Online Reservations

   The process by which tourists plan and book their travels has been completely transformed as a result of the advent of internet booking sites such as Expedia, Booking.com, and Airbnb. These platforms provide ease of use and openness in the process of making travel plans.

   5.2. Apps for Mobile Devices

   Travelers are becoming more reliant on mobile apps for everything from booking flights and accommodations to navigating, translating, and receiving recommendations in real time. Traveling in the present era requires the use of mobile apps more and more.

   5.3. Virtual Reality (VR) and Augmented Reality (AR) are both types of mixed reality

   Technologies such as virtual reality and augmented reality are being utilized in order to provide more immersive travel experiences. Before making reservations, vacationers can virtually investigate various travel options, including lodging, activities, and things to do.

   5.4. The Technology of Blockchain

   The blockchain technology is gaining interest in the travel sector because it offers safe and transparent payment mechanisms, as well as the potential for smart contracts that simplify the booking and travel procedures.

6. **Tourism in Outer Space**

   6.1 The Beginnings of Space Travel and Tourism

   The idea of people traveling across space for leisure or business purposes was formerly considered to be the realm of science fiction. Commercial space flight for private individuals is a goal that many corporations, like SpaceX and Blue Origin, are attempting to achieve.

   6.2. Flights Below the Orbit of the Earth

There is currently work being done to develop suborbital flights that will give passengers a taste of what it's like to journey to space. These flights provide passengers with a few minutes of weightlessness as well as breathtaking vistas of the planet below.

6.3. Tourism on the Moon and in Space Hotels

Travelers may one day have the possibility to stay in orbit or visit the Moon thanks to the development of the idea of space hotels and lunar tourism.

7. Difficulties and Things to Think About

7.1. Inequality in the Digital Age

There are some areas and communities that do not have the same level of access to the digital tools and platforms that are essential to the operation of modern tourism. The unequal access to digital resources can stifle economic expansion in certain regions.

7.2. Appropriation of Other Cultures and a Lack of Respect

There is a risk that tourists will accidentally harm the local culture, habits, and traditions, which might result in cultural conflicts and tensions.

7.3. Loss of Authenticity Due to Erosion

The expansion of virtual experiences and immersive technologies could result in a superficial awareness of destinations, which could potentially undermine the authenticity of travel.

7.4 Loss of Employment Opportunities

It is possible that jobs in conventional tourism sectors would be lost as a result of the proliferation of digital platforms and automation in the tourism business.

8. The Outlook for the Travel Industry

The future of travel will be characterized by a combination of these developing themes, with a heavy focus placed on sustainable travel, travel that emphasizes health and wellness, digital change, and, for some, the potential of traveling into space. This future holds many exciting potential for the tourism industry as a whole as well as for individual travelers, but it also poses issues that need to be addressed in order to ensure that tourism remains responsible and inclusive.

The changing preferences of tourists, developments in technology, and an increasing awareness of the need to be responsible to the environment and to society are all factors that are driving changes in the tourism industry. The travel and tourism sector is always evolving in response to the changing dynamics of the industry, which is influencing the future of travel as well as the kinds of experiences that travelers can anticipate having. In order to be successful in this shifting environment, the various stakeholders in the tourism sector need to embrace innovation, sustainability, and individualized experiences, while simultaneously tackling concerns linked to digital inequality, cultural sensitivity, and the preservation of authenticity. These new developments have the potential to reshape and improve the way in which we discover the world around us as they continue to emerge.

10.2 Technology's Impact on Tourism

Over the course of the last few decades, the travel and tourism industry has been subjected to a tremendous shift that has primarily been driven by developments in technology. Travelers now plan their trips, make reservations, and experience their trips very differently because to technological advancements such as internet booking platforms and virtual reality experiences. This essay examines the influence that technology has had on tourism as well as the ways in which it is influencing the future of travel.

1. **The Opening Statements**

    The worldwide tourist industry is undergoing a profound transformation as a direct result of the powerful influence of technology. Because of this, there have been substantial shifts not just for vacationers but also for the companies that cater to their needs in terms of research, planning, booking, and the overall experience of their visits. This essay explores the several ways in which technology has had an impact on the tourist industry and speculates on the ways in which it will continue to have an effect in the future.

2. **The Development of Technology Within the Tourism Industry**

   2.1. Platforms for Online Reservations

   Travelers now conduct their accommodation research and bookings in quite different ways because to the proliferation of internet booking sites such as Expedia, Booking.com, and Airbnb. These platforms provide passengers with booking methods that are both convenient and effective by offering a diverse selection of options, transparent pricing, and reviews written by other users.

   2.2. Applications for Mobile Devices

   Apps for mobile devices have rapidly become an indispensable resource for travelers. Mobile apps provide a variety of functionalities that enrich the trip experience. These functionalities range from booking flights and hotels to providing navigation, translation, and suggestions from locals.

   2.3. Virtual Reality (VR) and Augmented Reality (AR) are both types of mixed reality

   Technologies such as virtual reality and augmented reality have made it possible to create immersive experiences in the tourism industry. Before making reservations, vacationers can virtually investigate locations, lodging options, and things to do thanks to virtual reality (VR) technology. Augmented reality provides information and experiences in real time, both of which enhance traditional travel.

   2.4. The Technology of Blockchain

   The hospitality sector is one that is beginning to experience the impact of blockchain technology. It provides safe and transparent means of payment, does away with the requirement of currency exchange, and enables smart contracts, which simplify the processes of booking trips and making reservations.

3. **The Effect that Technology Has on Passengers**
   3.1. **Independent and Capable Travelers**
   Travelers now have access to an unprecedented amount of information and opportunities because to technological advancements. They have the ability to read reviews, conduct price comparisons, and study locations in order to make educated judgments.
   3.2. **Adaptation to the Individual**
   The use of data and algorithms by businesses to personalize customers' travel experiences in response to their unique tastes is made possible by advances in travel technology. Travelers are able to have more meaningful and enjoyable vacations thanks to individualized recommendations as well as individualized itineraries.
   3.3. **Travel That Is Effortless**
   Online check-ins, electronic boarding cards, and digital navigation aids that assist visitors in locating their way around unfamiliar locations are just a few examples of the ways in which technology has made travel more convenient and less cumbersome.
   3.4. **Communication in the Present Moment**
   Travelers are able to maintain relationships with their families and friends back home while they are away because to real-time communication technologies such as instant messaging apps. In addition to this, they make customer support and neighborhood recommendations very easy to obtain.
4. **Impact of New Technologies on Established Companies**
   4.1. **Heightened Publicity and Accessibility**
   Businesses have benefited from more visibility and a wider reach thanks to the rise of online booking platforms. Through the use of these channels, formerly inaccessible audiences can now be reached by individual hosts, local tour operators, and small boutique hotels.
   4.2. **Effectiveness of the Operations**
   Businesses in the tourism industry may now run their operations

more efficiently thanks to technological advancements. The use of centralized reservation systems, property management software, and tools for revenue management enables operations to be more efficiently optimized.

4.3. Analyses of the Data

Utilizing data analytics allows companies to acquire understanding into the behavior, tastes, and trends of customers who travel. Having access to this information enables them to make educated judgments on improvements to pricing, marketing, and overall customer experience.

4.4. Advertising and Public Relations

It is now imperative for tourism businesses to utilize digital marketing and social media in their promotional efforts. Businesses now have the ability to zero in on particular demographics and track the efficacy of their marketing efforts, both of which contribute to more successful advertising.

5. The State of the Art in Transportation Technology

5.1. Artificial Intelligence (AI)

The application of AI will become increasingly important in the travel industry. The use of chatbots, virtual assistants, and recommendations driven by AI will continue to advance and become more sophisticated in the next years, offering travelers with more individualized and convenient experiences.

5.2. IoT (Internet of Things)

The Internet of Things will improve the travel experience by providing an increased level of convenience and by linking tourists to the world around them. There will be an increase in the number of smart hotels, connected transit options, and wearable technologies.

5.3. Predictive Analytics and the Use of Big Data

The application of big data and predictive analytics will make it possible for businesses to anticipate the behavior of travelers and adjust their offerings accordingly. This will ultimately result in more efficient operations and better satisfaction among customers.

5.4. Environmental Responsibility and Clean Technology

The development of environmentally responsible tourism will be greatly aided by the application of technology. As more people look for environmentally conscious vacation options, green technologies like electric transportation and accommodations that are favorable to the environment will become increasingly common.

6. Obstacles and Things to Take Into Account

6.1. Inequality in the Digital Age

There are some areas and communities that do not have the same level of access to the digital tools and platforms that are essential to the operation of modern tourism. The unequal access to digital resources can stifle economic expansion in certain regions.

6.2. Personal Information and Safety

Privacy and safety concerns are becoming increasingly prominent as technological advancements become increasingly interwoven into the travel experience. It is necessary to protect the personal information of travelers, including the information on their passports and any payment details.

6.3. Appropriation of Culture and Sensitivity to Culture

Travelers who want to engage with local cultures through the use of technology run the risk of accidentally offending local practices and traditions. It can be difficult to find a happy medium between the two goals of cultural exchange and respect.

6.4. Displacement from One's Job

It is possible that jobs in conventional tourism sectors would be lost as a result of the proliferation of digital platforms and automation in the tourism business. Because of this shift, it is necessary to place an emphasis on retraining and expanding one's skill set for individuals who may be impacted.

The effect of technology on the tourism industry has been significant, and it will continue to play a role in determining the future of the sector. Businesses get better visibility, operational efficiency, and data analytics, while consumers gain the ability to make more informed decisions thanks to expanded access to information and more personalized experiences. The continual development of technology in the travel industry, driven by artificial intelligence (AI), internet of things (IoT), big data, and sustainable practices, promises even more interesting possibilities. However, it is vital for players in the tourism industry to address challenges linked to digital inequality, privacy, cultural sensitivity, and employment displacement. These issues are intertwined across the industry. By doing so, businesses will be able to leverage the power of technology to improve the quality of the travel experience while simultaneously supporting more responsible and environmentally friendly tourism.

10.3 Strategies for Sustainable and Inclusive Tourism

Tourism is a two-edged sword; on the one hand, it can create economic possibilities and foster cultural interaction, but on the other hand, it can also create environmental and social problems. It is necessary for tourism practices to be both sustainable and inclusive if they are to play a role in ensuring the long-term profitability of the tourism sector and the wellbeing of communities. This essay investigates different approaches that might be used in the tourist industry to achieve both sustainability and inclusion.

1. **The Opening Statements**

    Tourism that is sustainable and inclusive is an approach to travel that takes a comprehensive view of the industry, with the goal of limiting negative impacts while promoting positive outcomes for local communities, the environment, and travelers themselves. The goals of sustainable tourism are to preserve natural and cultural resources, lessen the impact on the environment, and bolster the economy of host communities. The concept of inclusive tourism places an emphasis on access and involvement for all individuals, irrespective of their physical capabilities, personal histories, or financial means. To accomplish these objectives, you will need to implement a number of different plans and programs.

2. **Methods for Creating a Tourism Industry That Is Sustainable**

   2.1. Planning and Management of Vacation Destinations

   It is essential to have efficient destination management in order to have sustainable tourism. This requires local governments, businesses, and communities to work together in order to build comprehensive plans that tackle concerns such as carrying capacity, infrastructure development, and resource conservation.

   2.2. Lodging Options That Are Friendly to the Environment

   Responsible tourism can be encouraged by promoting eco-friendly accommodations, such as hotels that have earned green certifications and are committed to sustainable operations. These companies lower their overall energy use, reduce the amount of garbage they produce, and support community efforts to improve the local environment.

   2.3. Participation in the Local Community

   It is essential to involve the local community in the planning and development of tourism. Communities are frequently the custodians of natural and cultural resources, and the input that they provide can drive the development of policies and activities that strike a balance between the priorities of inhabitants and those of tourists.

   2.4. Transportation That Is Sustainable

   The negative effects of tourism on the environment can be mitigated by encouraging the use of environmentally friendly modes of transportation, such as public transportation, bicycles, and electric vehicles. Congestion, pollution, and other problems related to overtourism are alleviated thanks to these choices, which also assist minimize congestion.

   2.5. Engaging with Wildlife in a Responsible Manner

Animals and their natural habitats can be protected from harm by participating in wildlife conservation programs and having responsible wildlife experiences, such as ethical animal interactions. It is imperative that tourists be made aware of the need of maintaining ethical conduct when interacting with wildlife.

3. **Methods for Creating an Inclusive Tourism Industry**

   3.1. Infrastructure That Is Accessible

   It is essential to provide accessible infrastructure in order to make tourism more inclusive. This includes ramps that are accessible for wheelchairs, restrooms that are appropriately equipped, and transportation alternatives that are handicapped-friendly so that individuals with disabilities can travel in comfort.

   3.2. Instruction and Consciousness

   It is imperative that those working in the tourism industry receive training on how to help travelers with impairments. This training should entail being sensitive to the needs of the individuals being trained as well as the usage of various assistive technologies.

   3.3. Marketing That Is Inclusive

   People of many ages, skills, and cultural origins should be featured in marketing initiatives that aim to be inclusive. This demonstrates that the location is friendly and accommodating to visitors of various backgrounds.

   3.4. Accessible Websites and Mobile Applications

   Websites and mobile applications pertaining to tourism need to be developed with accessibility in mind. This entails providing alternative language for images, allowing navigating via the keyboard, and being compatible with screen readers for users who have visual impairments.

   3.5. Activities and Attractions That Can Be Accessible

   It is important for tourist locations to provide attractions and activities that are accessible to persons of varying abilities and physical capacities. This may include tours that are conducted by audio, displays that can be touched, or interpretation in sign language.

4. Strategies That Dovetail Into One Another

4.1. Alignment of Sustainable Development and Inclusivity

Tourism that is both sustainable and inclusive typically goes hand in hand. For instance, eco-friendly accommodations may also have rooms and services that are accessible, making it possible for all kinds of guests to take pleasure in an environment that is both friendly and environmentally conscious.

4.2. Sensitivity to Cultural Aspects

Both environmentally responsible and inclusive tourism share the value of cultural awareness as an important factor. It is essential that tourists be made aware of how important it is to respect the cultures, customs, and traditions of the places they visit. This can help to avoid conflicts between different cultures and ensure that the cultural legacy of the place is maintained.

4.3. Contributing to the Strength of the Local Economy

Inclusion and sustainability both work toward the goal of supporting local economies. This can be accomplished by patronizing local establishments, working with local tour guides, and purchasing goods made from locally derived ingredients. In doing so, tourism can be made to be beneficial to the communities that it visits.

5. Obstacles and Things to Take Into Account

5.1. Keeping the Economic Interests

It can be difficult to strike a balance between the economic interests of tourism and other considerations, such as sustainability and inclusivity. Because tourism is frequently vital to the success of local economies, it is essential to strike a balance that is to the mutual advantage of all relevant parties.

5.2. Regulation and Administration of the Law

It can be difficult to enforce policies that are designed to encourage sustainable and inclusive tourism, which is especially true in regions that have fewer resources available for regulatory monitoring. For there to be success, there must first be effective policies and monitoring.

5.3. Sensitivity to Other Cultures

It can be difficult to demonstrate cultural sensitivity because it entails striking a balance between enabling tourists to participate in local traditions and preventing cultural appropriation and disrespect. This can be a difficult task. The most important things are education and awareness.

Tourism practices that are both sustainable and inclusive are essential to the long-term success of the tourism sector as well as the health and happiness of local communities and tourists. These practices incorporate a combination of measures, such as accessible infrastructure and inclusive marketing, destination management, and eco-friendly accommodations. Sustainable and inclusive tourism can contribute to the creation of a world in which travel is rewarding, respectful, and accessible to all people, despite the fact that there are problems to be faced. All that is required is the implementation of the appropriate policies, as well as a dedication to education and awareness. The tourist industry can continue to prosper while also protecting the locations that it visits if economic interests, environmental stewardship, and social responsibility are brought into alignment.

10.4 Preparing Local Economies for the Future

The health and resiliency of communities are directly influenced by the strength of their respective local economies. It is crucial to prepare local economies for the future as we traverse an era marked by fast breakthroughs in technology capabilities, challenges to the natural environment, and upheavals on a global scale. In order to ensure the financial well-being and overall vibrancy of local communities, it is necessary to encourage adaptation, sustainability, and inclusivity.

1. **The Spreading Out of Economic Activities**
   Many local economies are vulnerable to economic downturns because they are dependent on a particular industry or sector of the economy. This danger can be reduced by encouraging the growth of a diverse range of businesses within the community's economy. Promoting innovative thinking and entrepreneurial endeavors can contribute to the development of a more dynamic commercial environment. Fostering an environment that encourages economic variety requires a concerted effort on the part of governments, educational institutions, and business associations working together to provide assistance to new and aspiring business owners.

2. **Workforce Development and Training**
   It is imperative to educate and train the local labor force for the years to come. This includes making investments in education and training programs that provide individuals with the skills necessary to succeed in a labor market that is always shifting. A workforce that is both adaptive and competitive can be ensured when schools, vocational training centers, and local enterprises work together to develop educational programs. This can assist tailor educational programs to the specific needs of the community.

3. **Methods That Are Ecologically Sound**
   When it comes to getting local economies ready for the future, sustainability is one of the most important factors to take into account. Encouragement should be given to local firms to adopt environmentally friendly practices, cut down on waste, and lower their overall carbon footprint. Long-term environmental and economic sustainability can be helped along by actions in the areas of sustainable tourism, renewable energy initiatives, and conservation activities.

4. **Developments in Science and Industry**
   The combination of technological advancement and creative

thinking is absolutely necessary for the preparedness of regional economies for the future. In order to maintain connectivity and maintain a competitive edge, municipal governments had to make investments in digital infrastructure, such as high-speed internet and technology for smart cities. In addition, propelling local economies to the forefront of the digital age can be accomplished by cultivating innovation hubs, research centers, and partnerships with technology businesses.

5. **A Commitment to Equity and Inclusivity**
The process of future-proofing local economies should include inclusivity as a central component. It is not only a moral necessity but also a practical one to work toward the goal of providing equal access to economic opportunities for all people. Local economies have the ability to harness the full potential of their communities and achieve a workforce that is more robust and dynamic if they embrace diversity and promote equitable access to jobs, education, and assistance for entrepreneurs. This can be accomplished by fostering equality of access to these resources.

6. **Investment in Physical Infrastructure**
The creation of new physical infrastructure is an essential component of economic readiness. To ensure the smooth operation of local economies, infrastructure including roads, bridges, public transportation, and utilities are absolutely necessary. Investment in infrastructure not only results in the creation of new jobs, but it also contributes to economic expansion by enhancing connectivity and making the flow of products and services more straightforward.

7. **Cooperation Within the Region**
There is no such thing as a local economy that exists in a vacuum. It is crucial for economic resilience and growth to work together with the local governments and areas that are adjacent to your own. Partnerships at the regional level can result in economies of scale, shared resources, and cooperative infrastructure projects, all

of which can make an entire region more appealing to potential business owners and investors.

8. **Obtaining Financial Resources**

    Having access to cash is absolutely necessary for the development of new businesses and the growth of the economy. Entrepreneurs and enterprises should be provided with the required finance and financial support to drive growth and innovation through a collaborative effort on the part of local governments, financial institutions, and venture capital firms. This effort should take place.

9. **Contingency Planning and Response**

    It is important for regional economies to be ready for both economic and environmental catastrophes. Putting in place standards for risk assessment, disaster recovery systems, and contingency planning can be of assistance to local businesses and communities in the event of unforeseen interruptions.

10. **The Standard of Living**

The economic prospects of a region are substantially impacted by the quality of life in the region as a whole. A higher quality of life is achieved by investments in areas such as healthcare, education, public services, and cultural amenities. This, in turn, makes the region more appealing to both inhabitants and enterprises.

www.ingramcontent.com/pod-product-compliance
Lightning Source LLC
LaVergne TN
LVHW010159070526
838199LV00062B/4414